HEARTS ABLAZE

HEARTS ABLAZE

PARABLES FOR THE QUEER SOUL

ROLF R. NOLASCO JR.

Morehouse Publishing
NEW YORK

Unless otherwise noted, the Scripture quotations contained herein are from the New Revised Standard Version Bible, copyright © 1989 by the Division of Christian Education of the National Council of Churches of Christ in the U.S.A. Used by permission. All rights reserved.

Scripture quotations marked (NIV) are taken from the Holy Bible, New International Version®, NIV®. Copyright © 1973, 1978, 1984, 2011 by Biblica, Inc.™ Used by permission of Zondervan. All rights reserved worldwide. www.zondervan.com. The "NIV" and "New International Version" are trademarks registered in the United States Patent and Trademark Office by Biblica, Inc.™

Scripture quotations marked (NKJV) taken from the New King James Version®. Copyright © 1982 by Thomas Nelson. Used by permission. All rights reserved.

Morehouse Publishing, 19 East 34th Street, New York, NY 10016
Morehouse Publishing is an imprint of Church Publishing Incorporated.

Cover design by Dylan Marcus McConnell, Tiny Little Hammers
Typeset by Denise Hoff

Library of Congress Cataloging-in-Publication Data

Names: Nolasco, Rolf, 1967- author.
Title: Hearts ablaze : parables for the queer soul / Rolf Nolasco, Jr.
Description: New York, NY : Morehouse Publishing, [2022] | Includes
   bibliographical references.
Identifiers: LCCN 2022023033 (print) | LCCN 2022023034 (ebook) |
   ISBN 9781640653658 (paperback) | ISBN 9781640653665 (ebook)
Subjects: LCSH: Jesus Christ--Parables. | Christian sexual
   minorities--Religious life.
Classification: LCC BT375.3 .N65 2022 (print) | LCC BT375.3
   (ebook) | DDC 226.8/06--dc23/eng/20220725
LC record available at https://lccn.loc.gov/2022023033
LC ebook record available at https://lccn.loc.gov/2022023034

For all my Fab Queer Siblings,
especially Queer People of Color
who love fiercely,
regardless

&

Mama Lulu
who loves me,
just because

CONTENTS

INTRODUCTION

Queer Eye for
the Parables of Jesus

Queer Method

How might the very weapons used to clobber our queer spirit be used as a source of subversion and resistance to ignite our hearts and keep them ablaze, torches that will illumine the path for personal and collective queer liberation? Looking at the parables of Jesus with a queer eye is an attempt to answer that very question: it's a fresh take on these familiar parables intertwined with lived stories that I hope will be light for the journey.

I have written before about our queer identity with an approach of affirmation, naming us as God's Beloved Queers, with our manifold queer desires that include and yet transcend the erotic, and our human drive to flourish in all queer ways. This devotional book builds on that and then some. In a way, it's an exercise not simply of positivity, but a way of questioning the traditional, heteronormative readings of scripture and taking a particular queer approach.[1] I drew inspiration from queer biblical interpreters and their allies in continuing to center the experience and expertise of queer folk as both objects of affirmation and as subjects doing the interpretation.[2]

The impetus for this move is threefold. First, when we read biblical texts, we carry with us, albeit unconsciously for the most part, all that we are—our lived experiences as mediated by our gender, class, race, and everything that is descriptive of us over the course of our lives. These social descriptors are more than just frames we wear as we take our place and navigate the world in which we live. They are also the lenses through which we see the world and engage in it, through which these biblical texts are read, interpreted, and lived out. Every interpretation of biblical texts we hear and read is socially situated and constructed: gendered, sexed, raced, classed, and any other social category imaginable. Simply, we read, or better yet, interpret as we are. The texts, their translations, and subsequent interpretations are "not value-neutral but, rather, reflect to different degrees the relations and structures of race, gender, and class, which empower some persons and disenfranchise others" in the act of engaging these texts.[3] Hence, it might be helpful to ask the question—are the liberative purposes of God inhibited or unleashed as I or we encounter these texts?

On a much deeper level, this kind of interpretive engagement cultivates honesty in how we read the text and fosters humility in what we discover as we read. This could become an occasion for the cultivation of these human virtues, a process we are invited to participate in when we encounter and are encountered by the word and the Living Word. This critical, inclusive, and liberative approach to biblical interpretation assumes a partnership rather than a dominating and subjugating hierarchy that proliferates in most spaces we inhabit, either religious or otherwise.[4]

The objectivist approach—which means putting heavy emphasis on the claimed or assumed objectivity in historical-critical methods—has dominated biblical discourse for a long time and, in the process, has contributed to and sustained ongoing homophobic readings of scriptures that have caused much damage, harm, and trauma toward and in queer subjects and communities. Any act of interpretation is contingent, which means not objective.[5] That realization has emboldened "others-not-thought of"[6]—queer interpreters whose embodiment and deep desires can mine the truths that emerge at the intersection of queer lives and the "queer God."[7] As Timothy Koch puts it,

> We, as LGBT persons, come with our own questions, our own need for resources, our own limited energies: when we regard biblical texts as resources for us . . . we can find our own concerns, emotions, goals, and fears reflected through these pages; we

> can find role models, cautionary tales,
> ribald stories, and points to ponder
> that can illuminate our own journeys.[8]

After all, we too are direct recipients of God's unfolding new creation inaugurated by God in Jesus Christ, the Word-made-flesh who by his Spirit continues to disrupt our tendency to remain moored to the old, divisive, and passing man-made order. This book is a rendition of this new creation by lifting up queer voices not simply as hearers but as cointerpreters with the Living Word.

Second, since we are on the "inside of God's creative work," we can be playful, adventurous, imaginative, even messy at times, and hopefully transgressive (just look at chapter titles) in deciphering the meaning and significance of these texts for contemporary queer life. Here, I am blissfully provoked and inspired by queer interpreters who have engaged in midrash-making, an exegetical and close reading of the biblical text that is also "mystical, imaginative, revelatory, and, above all, religious."[9] Midrash-making follows the texts and opens up spaces between them for further interpretive work—for storytelling.[10] This license to generate meanings beyond, behind, and below the biblical texts gets a more focused yet playful treatment in our queer interpretation of the parables of Jesus, which are the heart of this devotional.

Third, I hope to nudge my queer siblings, especially those who have been burned, cut off, and demonized,

to reenter this liminal space of queer biblical interpretation. In this space, we are the protagonists, the
primary authors who will "re-define, re-describe,
and re-inscribe power" these texts in a manner that
will support and sustain the flourishing of our queer
lives.[11] More broadly, it is also a way of destabilizing
the damaging cis/hetero norm embedded in these
traditional readings often left undetected by unsus-
pecting and untrained eyes. When we are freed from
the constraints, regulation, censorship, and surveillance of our bodies, mind, and emotional life, we can
freely engage the text with an expectant heart of being
encountered by the Living Word, as we are. And for
many of us, this may be the first time to find ourselves
being spoken to as "objects within God's ken."[12] If so,
take delight in the knowledge that when we queer and
query these texts the treasure hidden in them reveals
itself for to us to (re)discover, reclaim, and enjoy.

As we venture into this expansive space of queer
imagination, we will be guided by the three-stage her-
meneutical arc put forth by Paul Ricoeur.[13] The distance between the world of the text, with its unique
social, cultural, and psychological contexts of the
author and its intended audience on the other side
and the unique world of the actual reader of the text,
then and now, is too wide, a chasm that is difficult to
bridge. The objectivist approach tries to narrow this
gap by focusing solely on the retrieval of the original,
unsullied, and intended meaning of the author, which
may serve the interest of the few and therefore eclipse

and subjugate further Christian queer persons or subjects who consider scriptural texts as potential sites for liberation. On the other hand, Ricoeur considers this gap—or *distanciation*, as he calls it—an open invitation for multiple interpretations so that a text becomes "inexhaustible in terms of reading . . . a world that opens up new possibilities of being."[14] The emphasis is placed on deciphering not the event itself but the multiple meanings behind it, which then offers queer interpreters a vast horizon on which to apply the text to the quotidian queer life. Ricoeur's three stages will serve as our lampposts in unearthing the treasures contained in the parables chosen for this devotional book.

The first stage is about the extraction of the meaning of the text as a whole, which in reality takes some guesswork because the text does not address us directly as readers and the author's intention is hard to ascertain and outside of our grasp. The focus of this task is to look at the text as more than a "linear sequence of sentences. It is a cumulative, holistic process . . . and opens them to plurality of constructions."[15] The second stage validates this guesswork by looking at the text from historically and critically oriented vantage points—that is, its particular historical and literary context—while bringing it into dialogue with our lives today.[16] The third stage is probably where the creative impulse of queer readers as bona fide interpreters reaches its peak, because in this stage we apply the meanings of the texts into our lives, making what was once alien familiar.[17]

I have engaged these parables from my position as a queer person of color. In a way, I have used a reader response approach, where the "reader makes their own meaning from the text that emphasizes their own particular responses to it."[18] I took seriously the socio-cultural and political contexts out of which the texts emerged, but they did not have the last word in what the parables mean. And neither do I. Queer biblical interpretation revels in constantly destabilizing any attempts to reach certainty and coherence. The difference that I hope I make is to center the particularities of queer life in the way I have experienced and embodied them and to use the texts to enrich and expand that life so that it flourishes.

My approach isn't a return to the nostalgic days of the ancient world, but a futuristic orientation in the sense that it orients readers to what is possible. It is ultimately about discerning the best way to respond to the *what* we find in the text. And what is possible is always open-ended, and what is proposed is simply that—a suggestion and not a final determination. This methodology opens up the possibility of liberating, compassionate, and subversive readings of the text. There is no better way to engage in this type of work than to queer the parables of Jesus, which as a literary device are already queer through and through. I call the fusion of queer methodology and the parables the "queerables of Jesus" because of their commitment to centering the lived experience of queer folk as a portal into the divine life.

Queerables of Jesus

Parables are like pride flags. They are diverse in forms (or colors), they are layered with possible meanings, yet they have a singular and symbolic intent to "convince and persuade." As a literary device, they are drawn from ordinary, real-life events that are made strange—queered—causing enough doubt to make us really think about what is going on. In other words, parables create an opening for the reader to see the world with fresh eyes so the story can "deceive them into truth." They are "truths in drag"—they draw or tease us into the story that is familiar, vivid, and strange (like a drag performance) and then leave us there bewildered and astonished enough to "awaken insight, stimulate the conscience, and move to action."[19]

The parables of Jesus reflect all these characteristics. They are so well known some of them have entered the vernacular (think of the word *prodigal*, for example), have been rendered into beautiful masterpieces (like Vincent van Gogh's *The Good Samaritan*), and most of all have been appropriated as lampposts to cast light on the journey of faith. But Jesus's parables are very queer in their attempts at evoking both "delight and instruction to countless people and offense to others," perhaps offensive to those who refused to have their version of reality be interrogated and disturbed. This is where Jesus's parables become even more subversive, because "Jesus used [parables] more frequently to explain the kingdom of God and to show the character of God and the expectations that God has for humans." The religious elite then and now have always shivered at the thought of Jesus inaugurating a radical vision of a world (reign, kin-dom, or queerdom of God) that is not run by a system of power and privilege. In some ways, these parables are an indictment of this spiritual form of elitism, a challenge to a lite and sanitized reading, and a source of encouragement to those who want to read them out of a liberationist framework or freedom from various forms of oppression—from personal to social to political, economic, and spiritual.[20]

The ten queerables I offer here are articulations of that framework. Personally, these parables have served as my anchor as I grappled with my own sexuality and gender identity and burgeoning faith very early on in my life. Amid the torrent of hateful and harmful messages that circulated, these queerables have provided respite and reassurance of God's unconditional and expansive love. I hope you will find shelter and nourishment in them, as well. Chapter 1, "TLC" (The Parable of the Good Shepherd, John 10:1–5), positions queer folk as sheepfold who receive some TLC, or tender loving care, by the Good Shepherd. Chapter 2, "Don't Forget to RSVP" (The Parable of the Great Banquet, Luke 14:16–24), declares the gratuitous character of the love of God that cannot be contained by politics nor church polity. As image-bearers of God, queer folk are invited to partake in and enjoy a generous helping of nourishment in the banquet with Christ as host. Chapter 3, "The Queerdom of God" (The

Parable of the Mustard Seed, Mark 4:30–32), admonishes queer followers of Christ seeking shelter in the queerdom of God to remain steadfast in their faith, which, like a mustard seed, has grown and continues to provide a sacred canopy and inspiration to others on the journey. Chapter 4, "Queer Joy" (The Parable of the Hidden Treasure, Matthew 13:44), describes in detail the experience of joy evoked by the discovery of the queerdom of God. This joy—better yet, queer joy—demands that we drop all so we gain all. Chapter 5, "Q-Connections" (The Parable of the Sower, Matthew 13:3–8), explores the role of the queer community in the active reception of the Word. This beloved community, with its rich soil, creates a habitat vital for queer flourishing. The task of queer followers of Christ is to cultivate our inner life—the interior garden of the soul—so our outer life radiates the light of Christ that is in us.

Chapter 6, "Queer Bodies" (The Parable of New Wine in Old Wineskins, Luke 5:37–39), is a meditation on what it means for our material, corporeal, queer flesh (new wineskin) to become a vessel for the ongoing liberative purposes of God in Jesus Christ for all of creation (new wine). Chapter 7, "Queer Father" (The Parable of the Lost Son, Luke 15:11–32), helps us ponder what it means for us to be like the queer father, mother, or parent and to allow this queerness to imbue our ways of being with others so that when the offer of love is rejected or missed, we can still choose to love that person regardless. Chapter 8,

"Neighborly Love" (The Parable of the Good Samaritan, Luke 10:25–37), recasts queer folk as good Samaritans to those hurting—from individual relations to faith communities—out of the depths of pain we have endured both from the hands of robbers and religious communities. Chapter 9, "Queers' Got Talent" (The Parable of the Talents, Matthew 25:14–30), celebrates and affirms the charisms of queer folk as integral to the life and mission of the church. By regarding us as trustworthy servants entrusted with talents and gold, we become active participants in the flourishing of others who make up the body of Christ. Chapter 10, "Queer Christ" (The Parable of the Wise and Foolish Builders, Luke 6:47–49), circles back to where the book started—an admonition to remain grafted to the True Vine, to listen attentively to the Good Shepherd, to stand on the chief cornerstone, the queer Christ. By standing on this sure foundation, queer folk are anchored firmly and fiercely amid the daily and unremitting challenges and obstacles that will continue to come our way.

The book ends with an epilogue—an adaptation of a sermon I preached soon after the Special General Conference of the United Methodist Church took place in St. Louis, Missouri, in February 2019 that banned queer UMC clergy from exercising their sacred call and curtailed their human and divine right to embody their sexuality and gender identity in their fullness. It was my way of reflecting on the damage and harm committed against my queer UMC clergy siblings and working to embolden their fierce love, regardless of circumstance. It feels like a fitting way to wrap things up.

To make our queer reading more accessible, I have included fragments of stories of queer United Methodist Church clergy whom I have had the privilege to sit with and interview as part of a grant I received from the Louisville Institute. This project was meant to describe and represent the subjective and deeply personal experience and action of these ordained ministers of the gospel who are staying on course, fulfilling their sacred call expressed in manifold forms while enduring what is tantamount to sacred violence. Their stories bring such a rich dimension to these queerables, which I hope will set our hearts ablaze and ignite our queer spirit.

Let's gather around the queer flame. Inspired by the ballroom scene, our "dress up" category or theme is Queers on Fire.

CHAPTER 1

TLC

The Parable
of the Good Shepherd

John 10:1–5

Very truly, I tell you, anyone who does not enter the sheepfold by the gate but climbs in by another way is a thief and a bandit. The one who enters by the gate is the shepherd of the sheep. The gatekeeper opens the gate for him, and the sheep hear his voice. He calls his own sheep by name and leads them out. When he has brought out all his own, he goes ahead of them, and the sheep follow him because they know his voice. They will not follow a stranger, but they will run from him because they do not know the voice of strangers.

This short meditation renders queer folk as sheepfold who receive some TLC, or tender loving care, by the Good Shepherd.

"We don't ask, and you don't tell us" is a phrase June heard repeatedly from folks involved in her ordination process early on, and she is "tired . . . very tired" of hearing it. It wasn't the first time she had been warned to hide her sexuality, to not speak of her truth, to not let her authentic self come out in her quest to listen and respond to God's call on her life.

Growing up in a very conservative environment, June was already conditioned to believe, through constant and consistent messaging from the pulpit, that her sexuality conflicted with her faith. Deep down she knew her "church would not give an answer, and the Bible too does not give a clear answer on these issues." But she was unrelenting. Her inner voice, though faint and often drowned out by a cacophony of lies, guided her. She set out on an adventure to discover a path that would help her reconcile these two important and fluid aspects of her identity.

> I thought studying theology would help, but that did not yield much helpful information, as the school I went to was so male centered. I moved to an all-women's college, and there I was introduced to feminist theology, which cracked open a new path for me. I

thought, *If I go this direction, I may find something that will counteract the message I have been hearing all these years.* Everybody says it is not God's will, but deep in my heart I don't think God is really against it.

June heard the voice and knew who it was.

The Shepherd's Voice

The parable of the good shepherd in John 10:1–5 holds the familiar theme of hearing and knowing a particular voice amid the noise, exacerbated by the presence of thieves and strangers. Before we reveal the parable's queer potential, Avedis Boynerian offers an up-close and personal account of shepherding in the Middle East.

Early each morning the flock starts to get excited because they have had nothing to eat for fourteen hours or more. In addition to being hungry, they are restless from being cooped up all night. As daylight increases, they gradually become more and more active and eager. Finally, they hear the shepherd's voice outside the barred sheepfold door. As soon as the door is opened by a member of the family, the shepherd calls the animals again and they rush out eagerly anticipating a new day full of lush grass, fresh mountain air, shady trees, and rest beside peaceful waters. The new sheep runs around and around banging its head against the rough stone walls of the sheepfold emitting a stream of pitiful, heartbreaking cries. It needs a few days of "therapy" to retrain its ear to recognize the voice of the new shepherd.[1]

With this as a backdrop, let us explore the queerable (queering the parable) of the good shepherd in John 10. We will focus on the first five verses, though we will look at the rest of the parable to deepen our queer commentary.

The parable starts with a threat from outside—from a thief "who does not enter the sheepfold by the gate but climbs in by another way" (v. 1). During those times, the shepherd faced threats from thieves and strangers, who were a danger everywhere, and from wild animals.[2] The thief's sole mission was to steal a sheep by force by climbing over the wall of the sheepfold at night when everyone is asleep. They might come with a ladder and a plan of operation, or with an accomplice to make a quick steal and escape. Often, the operation was violent because thieves had one purpose in mind: to "steal and kill and destroy" (v. 10). Queer folk have fallen in the hands of these kinds of people and have suffered a similar plight with frightening regularity.

The other potential human threat is a "stranger" (v. 5). Though not a thief, the stranger could cause noise, confusion, and disruption because their call was unfamiliar; theirs was an unrecognizable voice, especially for the young sheep—a voice that could lead to harm, even death and destruction. Hence, the sheep ran away because they did not recognize the stranger's voice. The inclusion of the stranger in the parable is a way of unveiling those considered strangers in Jesus's time: "the sectarians outside Jericho, the high priestly guild in the temple, and the scribes and Pharisees . . . Hellenists, the Herodians, Zealots and Sadducees."[3] Queer folk, due to their vulnerability, internalized homophobia and transphobia, and a longing to belong and be accepted, have been co-opted, tokenized, used, and abused by those whose intent is to further their cis/heterosexist agenda.

Carefully inserted between the thief and the stranger is the good shepherd whose portrayal in the parable evokes familiarity, intimacy, and faithful accompaniment. Unlike the thief who climbed over the wall or the stranger who caused confusion, the shepherd went straight through the door of the sheepfold in broad daylight. No escape plan or manipulative ruse, just a simple, regular, and ordinary trek to the sheepfold. Verse 3, which includes a short and to-the-point description, provides a clear characterization of the good shepherd.

The sheep hear his voice [familiarity].
He calls his own sheep by name [intimacy]
and leads them out [faithful accompaniment].

The voice of the shepherd is central to this parable. Shepherds called out with a chant, using a bam-
boo flute, or, most commonly, a simple cry, "Haa, haa,
ta'o, ta'o."[4] The flock heard, recognized, and rested in
the familiarity of the unique tone and resonance of the
shepherd's voice. Other herders might have sung the
same familiar tune, but the sheep knew the particular
timbre that caused their ears to perk up.

For the shepherd to lead and care for their flock,
the sheep had to hear and follow, but the scenario is
anything but simple because the sheep were often
mixed in among other flocks whose shepherds had
varying calls.[5] It was chaotic and loud and busy in the
narrow streets of those Palestinian villages, yet the
sheep had sharp ears and would only follow the voice
of their own shepherd.

This familiarity was further deepened by the shepherd calling his sheep by name (v. 3). The bond was
unmistakable and the connection as real as those we
witness or expect of intimate human relations—there
is liking, even favoritism and delight to make the other
person feel special and significant: "Some sheep always
keep near the shepherd and are his special favorites.
Each of them has a name, to which it answers joyfully,
and the kind shepherd is ever distributing to such
choice portions which he gathers for that purpose."[6]

The naming made proximity to the shepherd easier, if not inevitable, and also revealed the shepherd's abiding presence, deep regard, sensitive care, and intimate knowledge of his flock.

The familiarity and intimacy gave rise to the shepherd's next move—leading them out: "When he has brought out all his own, he goes ahead of them, and the sheep follow him because they know his voice" (v. 4). The good shepherd did not use force to keep the sheep moving in a particular direction or impatiently go far ahead of his flock, leaving them abandoned, lost, or scattered. He led them out, all of them out; not one was left behind, because he was an intentional, careful, and gentle shepherd. He went on ahead, neither too close nor too far, but just enough so the flock could still hear his distinct voice clearly and follow him into the vast wilderness in search of green pastures. This faithful accompaniment provided assurance of the shepherd's abiding presence throughout the journey and unwavering trust that he would lead them to a pasture where they could graze, drink, and rest. The parable shows that attending to the flock's well-being is at the heart of what it means to be a good shepherd.

The Queer Flock

Queer folk can glean (or graze) many life parallels from this parable (or pasture). Let's start with the traditional title—the Good Shepherd. Eight texts in the Bible identify the shepherd: four times in the Hebrew Bible referring to God (Psalm 23; Jeremiah 23; Ezekiel 34; Zechariah 10) and four times in the New Testament referring to Christ (Matthew 18; Mark 6; Luke 15; John 10). God or Christ as the Good Shepherd occupied the imagination of the early church, which is often depicted as the "religion of the Good Shepherd. The kindness, the courage, the grace, the love, the beauty of the Good Shepherd was to them, if we may so say, Prayer Book and Articles, Creeds, and Canons, all in one."[7] In their hearts and minds, they saw and experienced the nearness and tender care of God.

Interestingly, the image of the good shepherd (along with such symbols as the fish and the vine) almost disappeared after the fourth century and was replaced with dogmas and decrees. Instead of the image of the shepherd that suggested "the recovery of the lost sheep, the tender care and protection, the green pasture and fresh foundation, the sacrifice of life: in a word the whole picture of a Savior,"[8] having the right belief or doctrine took center stage; doing rightly receded to the background.

The dominant divine image that most queer folk have from the pulpit and other religious spaces when talking (or writing) about human sexuality is a queer-hating, cis/hetero-affirming, masculine-worshipping, judgmental, and punitive God who sends queer folk to hell for being ungodly—meaning, not straight. This parable recovers the ancient and much needed image of a God and Christ who tend for and accompany us ever so intentionally, gently, and faithfully through the maze that is life. It is an image of presence, not punishment.

• • •

"I started talking to God about my sexuality when I was in fifth grade," June reminisced. "I knew that I liked girls. I was even attracted to one of my female friends. Of course, I was afraid back then because I was taught to believe it wasn't normal to feel this way, and I talked to God about it. I actually talk to God a lot, like a friend."

I could feel a sense of freedom and lightness as June shared this part of her story. Contrary to what she was told during her ordination process—"we don't ask, you don't tell us"—she felt she could be unabashedly honest and candid with God. In a way, she was buoyed by this unspoken invitation—"just tell me and I will listen"—that freed her to simply be, as she is, in the presence of God.

Like the flock in the parable, June finds the image of God as the Good Shepherd very safe. At a very young age, she heard the nonjudgmental and familiar voice of God. Even in the cacophony of lies and the vitriolic speech that proliferates cis/hetero spaces, she discerned rather starkly the still, small, and gentle voice of God affirming all that she is without conditions, erasures, or censorship. And that was enough for her to express her heart's desire, ask lingering questions and address fear about her burgeoning sexuality, and perhaps lean into a childlike faith and resistance against imposters.

There are people and communities who steal queer joy by repeatedly arousing fear and expressing the disgust inherent in the normative discourse on human sexuality. And they do so strategically, with destructive and often fatal consequences. The same message of condemnation is directed at queer folk time and time again. This incessant messaging comes with the invocation of the sacred: it is God's will that we all be heterosexuals. The thief wears a "holy garb" and utters "holy speech" as a way of regulating erotic desires and privileging cis/heteronormativity.

Second, this hetero-talk comes with an emotional booster, disgust that elicits a combination of physical and behavioral aversive reactions. Since queer life is labeled by some as a moral offense, it generates "avoidance of disgust treats" that put queer folk in vulnerable and precarious situations.[9] Pairing vitriolic speech with disgust is a way of pushing the source of "unpleasantness away to a more comfortable psychological distance" that often leads to death, profound bodily injury, or "moments which position queer subjects as failed in their failure to live up to the heterosexual norm."[10]

Then come those who sing the same tune as the good shepherd, but their voice is too strange for the sheep to follow. Here, queer inclusion is half-hearted and often only for appearance's sake. In other words, queer folk are tokenized. These strangers use the same song—progressive and persuasive words of inclusion—yet task queer subjects to carry the heavy burden of justice making. Worse, rewards and recognition are often doled out to institutions with inclusionary practices, while behind closed doors, we witness fatigued, overutilized (and often underpaid), and even harassed queer folk. Simply, the flock's needs and well-being are verbally promised but not usually delivered.

Not so with the Good Shepherd, whose proximity is closer than we think and whose affections toward us remain steadfast and assured. I take the shepherd's act of naming his sheep in the parable as God's naming or calling us into existence. Our Good Shepherd breathes life into our queerness—excitedly anticipating our flourishing, even facilitating its fruition—for we bear the image of God in every queer way (v. 10). Remember this: we are not defective heterosexuals, but icons of the "Triune God just like everyone else, a window into the spacious gratuitous and transforming love of God."[11]

There's another dimension to this intimacy that we know quite well as God's queer flock, which June poignantly captured when she expressed, "In the midst of this pain we can meet God because God is with us when we are in pain." That has been her testimony, and I am sure it is the same for other countless queer folk whose lives are marked by incalculable pain and trauma because of who we are and whom we love. The image of a shepherd carrying a wounded sheep on

his shoulder to ease the pain and make easier the journey to healing and recovery comes to mind so vividly
when I visualize this image.

Christ, the Good Shepherd, goes further than
merely providing us tender loving care during those
dark and painful moments. He goes ahead of the
sheep (v. 4) and "lays down his life for the sheep" (v.
11), which in christological terms is very significant.
The kenotic or self-emptying hymn in Philippians
2 describes Christ's unsettling but liberating identification with us, a paradigmatic example of utter
dispossession:

> [Christ], being in very nature God, did
> not consider equality with God some
> thing to be used to his own advan
> tage; rather, he made himself nothing
> by taking the very nature of a servant,
> being made in human likeness. And
> being found in appearance as a man,
> he humbled himself by becoming obe
> dient to death—even death on a cross!
> (vv. 6–8, NIV)

In other words, he willingly subjected himself to
extreme humiliation by occupying the place of shame
(a common experience for queer folk), not to appease
God's vengeful intentions but to make plain our own
tendency for violence. He did not accomplish all this
to shame us or make us feel guilty, but to grant us

unqualified forgiveness so we can begin to live differently and truly treat each other as image bearers of a loving, forgiving, and compassionate God.[12]

This may be difficult to grasp, especially for those of us whose experience of the divine is mediated by thieves and strangers dressed as shepherds. There is no judgment from the true Shepherd who weeps at the sight of his wounded queer flock and who desires only our healing and freedom from the shackles of sacred violence that is cis/heteronormativity. And so, wherever we are in this journey, Christ's love for us precedes, transcends, and is beyond all that deters us from flourishing. Even at our weakest moments, the shepherd's forgiving heart, tender loving care, and gaze remain unchanged because God's only intention for God's queer flock is to heal our fragmented selves, help us remember our sacred worth, restore our place in the queerdom, and bring us back to the sheepfold.

This healing and hope is not reserved only for the few; the shepherd leads them *all* out (v. 3). No one is left behind, scattered, abandoned, or lost—a different story from the way the heterosexist world operates. In their attempt to control, surveil, and regulate the queer community, the heterosexist world has created a sexual identity framework that divides people into two warring groups. The "in group" (heterosexual) has distinguishable notions of order, goodness, and moral superiority, and the "out group" (gender and sexual minority) is deemed to have fallen from sacred favor and grace and therefore deserves death and destruction.

But the Good Shepherd will not go ahead of the flock until *everyone* is accounted for, until *everyone* gets a sit at the table, until *everyone* is affirmed, deployed, and celebrated as a key figure in the religious life of the faith community. Sometimes we cry out, "Come, Lord Jesus, come" as the pain, trauma, and exclusionary practices are too overwhelming to bear, work through, and address. Indeed, the struggle is real and often comes with material, even fatal, consequences. But as we listen to the voice of the Good Shepherd, we can hope that Christ's descent toward the "downward path of dishonor, suffering, and self-renouncing love"[13] is also his way of entering the depths of human vulnerability and, by extension, directly experiencing the very depths of our woundedness.

He is also searching for those of us who have been exiled and scattered, like a shepherd who will not leave until all have come out (and coming out, in whatever form and time this may take, is an important part of queer self-assertion). And when our bruised and broken selves are found by our Good Shepherd, he will feed and care for us, hold us with comfort, tender loving care, and focused intent to heal and restore us. Perhaps, as he carries us on his shoulders, we can lean into the "voice of God, the creator and holder in being, the love and gatherer of the weak, a voice far too quiet to be able to be heard in the midst of all that wrath of spurned love."[14]

The struggle for LGBTQIA+ inclusion within June's denomination looms large. And yet, amid all this, June has found hope and inspiration from her queer siblings and allies who told her that she will be appointed to a reconciling church and that she has her bishop's support in all of this. This gave her much-needed assurance and confirmation of God's call on her life: "I just want a church that I could pastor. I feel called to this. I am not in ministry only for LGBTQ equality. I am a pastor who happens to be a lesbian, and so if I am in a church who sees no issue with the pastor who happens to be a lesbian, then I'd be happy to serve."

The sheep who has been lovingly and faithfully shepherded by the Good Shepherd is now ready to provide this same tender loving care toward her own flock.

So, let the queer flock gather and our theme or category is: Give us some TLC, or Tender Loving Care.

CHAPTER 2

DON'T FORGET TO RSVP

The Parable of the Great Banquet

Luke 14:16–24

Then Jesus said to him, "Someone gave a great dinner and invited many. At the time for the dinner he sent his slave to say to those who had been invited, 'Come; for everything is ready now.' But they all alike began to make excuses. The first said to him, 'I have bought a piece of land, and I must go out and see it; please accept my regrets.' Another said, 'I have bought five yoke of oxen, and I am going to try them out; please accept my regrets.' Another said, 'I have just been married, and therefore I cannot come.' So the slave returned and reported this to his master. Then the owner of the house became angry and said to his slave, 'Go out at once into the

streets and lanes of the town and bring
in the poor, the crippled, the blind, and
the lame.' And the slave said, 'Sir, what
you ordered has been done, and there
is still room.' Then the master said to the
slave, 'Go out into the roads and lanes,
and compel people to come in, so that
my house may be filled. For I tell you,
none of those who were invited will taste
my dinner.'"

*The gratuitous and diffusive character of the love of God
cannot be contained either by politics or church polity.
As image-bearers of God, like everyone else, queer folk
are invited to partake in and enjoy a generous helping of
nourishment at the banquet with Christ as host.*

Unwanted Guests

Carrying a basketful of vegetables, Rume ran hurriedly to the kitchen to meet his mom, Lucy, who was
the cook in charge for a party her older sister, Linda,
was throwing. The place was buzzing, and everyone
looked stressed, including Lucy. When she saw Rume,
she breathed a sigh of relief and grabbed the basket;
she laid all the vegetables for her famous *kare-kare* in
the kitchen sink and started rinsing them. Sensing his
mom needed help, Rume took over at the sink so she
could start cutting the vegetables.

Soon after, Lucy asked him to get the broom from
the garage and sweep the kitchen floor. On his way

there, he ran into Linda in a flowy, flowery dress, a pair of nude sandals, and dangling pearl earrings. With a face covered in branded makeup, she looked at Rume and with sternly voice said, "Make sure that you don't eat with my guests."

Stunned, Rume lowered his face and said, "Yes, Auntie." He kept the brief encounter to himself. The guests happened to be Linda's and Lucy's relatives, and therefore Rume's as well, except that everyone but Rume and his mother belonged to *alta ciudad*—that is, they were monied and well known in their clan. Honor and shame were simultaneously disbursed according to status in life.

I am sure this happens a lot in society, where social stratification is rigidly observed and enforced—even among blood relations. It occurs with horrifying frequency in the Philippines, with its daily afternoon TV soap operas mirroring real life; in willful exaggeration or crude caricature this sad truth is not lost on many *Pinoys*.

And then there's the ordinary table gathering, where a seat at the table is cordoned off or stratified and reserved for those who fit cis/heterosexual norms. Queer folk, especially queer youth, have not been given these seats, usually by their own family, mostly on religious grounds. This stretches to the eucharistic table, where queer clergy are barred from participating in, let alone officiating at, this intimate table fellowship in conservative religious spaces. Honor and shame are simultaneously disbursed according to gender norms.

Unexpected Guests

Sandwiched between a short narrative about Jesus dining at a Pharisee's house (Luke 14:1–15) and his frank directive about what it means to follow him (Luke 14: 25–35) the parable of the great banquet highlights the theme of honor (God's display of overflowing generosity toward those who are considered unworthy and undeserving) and shame (God's indictment of those overtaken by worldly preoccupations and chained in their perceived and enacted power and privilege).

The abundant display of open-handedness through healing and honor giving is aimed quite specifically at the "poor, the crippled, the lame, and the blind" (vv. 13, 21). In the face of a heavily stratified social order and all the perks that come with being part of the "in group," this parable offers a divine alternative order that centers, privileges, and honors the have-nots— those long kept outside of or on the periphery of the haves, those folks with status, influence, power, and material possessions. Simply, this parable discloses another way of being in the world, one that challenges and inverts the prevailing lifeworld and calls for a "fundamental reorientation" toward a world *otherwise*.[1]

Let's queer the parable in detail.

The story starts with an invocation from one of the guests at the Pharisee's house—"Blessed is anyone who will eat bread in the kin-dom of God" (v. 15)— which introduces the subject of eating in the kin-dom of God as a way of foreshadowing a great and final banquet at the end of history. The image of eating a sacred meal with God, of feasting on rich foods and wines, at the end times was well known among the Jews. In Psalm 23:5 and Isaiah 25:6–9, God is the host of this great banquet, giving honor to all the peoples and nations based purely on grace and overflowing generosity; the participants from the nations bring nothing.[2] The pious guest might have had this in the back of his mind when he uttered the invocation.

This exchange between Jesus and the diner (vv. 14–15) is a fascinating reversal of the social ladder that would have easily threatened the position the privileged had firmly established for themselves. What would become of them at the eschatological banquet? Remember that these are the same folks for whom obedience to purity laws was paramount and who considered themselves unblemished and worthy of a seat at the table. Would they get an invitation to the banquet as well? Who would be on the guest list in the first place? Who was off the list? And what list was being used: the old-world order or the new one inaugurated by the Messiah? The pious diner seems to have an answer, and quite a confident answer at that. Those whom Jesus mentioned in verse 13 and again in verse 21 were the ones who would have seats at the banqueting table: the "poor, the crippled, the lame, and the blind." But just in case this reversal of the old-world order in the eschatological age was missed, Jesus offered the parable at hand.

At the center of the story is a "certain man" who was preparing "a great banquet" for his invited friends and associates. The social practices and etiquette of the traditional Middle Eastern context were at play. A double invitation was sent to each guest: the first one to ensure that the invitation was given to the right person, and the second sent at the hour of the banquet to confirm their presence and let them know that "everything is ready now" (v. 17). Those listening to the first two lines of the parable may have wondered, "If the hour of the banquet was approaching, invitations had gone out, and all was ready, those who had seats at the table must have been hurrying to "feast and enjoy the fellowship and nourishment of the long anticipated repast."[3]

Not so fast; the parable takes an unexpected turn. Instead of hurrying to eat, the invited guests all made excuses, which in that culture (or any culture, for that matter) was a grave insult, an act of great discourtesy, to the host. And worse, the reasons given by the guests were outright lies. Everyone in first-century Palestine would have known it. No one bought land without knowing every little detail about the piece of property. No one bought a team of oxen without first watching how they worked in the field. And no one in the village would have two grand occasions at once, because everyone would have been at the wedding, perhaps including the host of the party. Their excuses were total fabrication, rude and crude ways of showing how they truly felt about their friend, the host. In the brief exchanges, their true preferences and loyalties were made visible. For them, possessions took priority over the person. And in a society in which personal relationships mattered the most, they decided to "unfriend" themselves, something that "strikes with special force"[4]—an ultimate form of betrayal.

The servant came back and reported what had transpired. The banquet host was livid upon hearing all this, and rightly so. Not only was he publicly insulted, he had also been taken for a fool. What happened next, though, is the surprising point of the parable. The invitation to the banquet, spurned by the haves, was extended to the have-nots—those without influence and power, those pushed to the margins, those ostracized and undeserving of honor by the world's standards (v. 21). The guests of honor were the poor who were never invited to parties, the blind who did not go out to examine the field, the lame who could not test oxen, and the maimed who did not get married.[5] Their acceptance of the invitation stands in clear juxtaposition to the dishonest refusal of their well-to-do counterparts. And the message is clear: attendance at the banquet is solely based on the response to the invitation, not on who receives it.

The last two lines underscore the host's diffusive generosity, an "unexpected visible demonstration of love in humiliation." He expanded the circle of the guests of honor to include those beyond the town's immediate vicinity, going out into "roads and lanes" (v. 23) "along which beggars might rest for protection."[6]

It also hints at what's going to happen to those who rejected the invitation in the first place. Their shameful acts will be meted out with equally stern declaration; "none of those who were invited will taste my dinner" (v. 24).

Curiously, a shift has occurred, from Jesus narrating the story to directly addressing the crowd in the Pharisee's house with the words, "I tell you . . ." (and by extension addressing everyone reading the parable at every age). The theological significance of Jesus's I-statement is that his presence inaugurated the arrival of the kin-dom of God; he is the host of the banquet. He is the one who extends the invitation to the undeserving and bestows honor on them for their acceptance. In a sense, Jesus exhibits a "preferential option for the poor,"[7] which he lived out unapologetically by regularly sharing table fellowship with tax collectors and sinners. Put another way, he makes possible for us to come under God's care and reign, to be true heirs of the kin-dom.

The inverse is true as well. Those who refuse and make excuses, just like the guests in the parable, incur for themselves a self-imposed judgment and shame, shut off from intimate fellowship with the host and his guests. For in Jesus, "the eschatological age has dawned. Respond to the invitation or opt out of participation in God's salvation."[8]

Guests of Honor

Queer folk reading this parable, take this to heart and make no mistake: God's queer, gentle, and delightful gaze is directed toward us. Our names are on the list, for we are guests of honor in God's banqueting table. That may come as a surprise or be hard to understand. For the longest time, our queer life has been weaponized against us, used as a mark to cement our place as outsiders, undeserving of any divine favors or barred from inhabiting sacred spaces to live out our calling, and our path is considered a sure road to hell. Basking in their cis/heterosexual glory, some are certain that there is no way for us to be invited to the banquet because the honor only belongs to them. To legitimize this, they have co-opted the name of God to dim or snuff out the divine light that is sparkling within us. And yet, no matter what they do or what they say, the fact remains that you and I, along with our queer siblings, have been summoned and invited to make an appearance at God's own soiree. A table was reserved for us long before we realized our true sacred worth and long after the self-proclaimed keepers of God's kin-dom realize their grave mistake.

As recipients of God's abundance, preference, and sacred call, our acceptance of the invitation is also an acceptance of a life befitting our identity as God's Beloved Queers. This involves three movements and intentions: first, going inward with the intention to nurture a life of interiority; second, going outward with the intention to further God's work of inclusion;

and third, going upward with the intention to live the demands of discipleship.

The movement inward can be arduous and painful. The relentless words of disapproval we hear and exclusionary practices we are subjected to cleave onto our psyche like superglue. We have become so wedded to these experiences that they have produced negative self-talk and perhaps driven us toward self-destructive behaviors. We have become our own worst enemies. Part of tending our inner life is to be aware of these insidious dynamics and remember that these critical voices are not our own; these practices of exclusion are projections based on fear, ignorance, and an effort to maintain power and to control our bodies and erotic desires. Through the hard but ultimately rewarding work of deepening our self-awareness, we can begin to unclasp our psyche from the chains of internalized trans- and homophobia. By venturing into personal therapy or spiritual direction, encircling ourselves with people who will remind us of our worth and pick us up when we slip, and practicing self-compassion we can begin clearing all the toxins that cling to our psyche.

Let me be clear, though. We don't have to have it all together or consider ourselves enlightened, woke, or therapy saturated to show up at the banquet or enter the kin-dom of God. Health—whether physical, psychological, or spiritual—is not a prerequisite. Acceptance of the invitation is all that is required. Remember that the "poor, the crippled, the blind, and the lame" in the parable showed up as they were. And we can do the same. However, the internal and personal work we are committing ourselves to engage in will unleash the fullness of life promised to us as heirs of the kin-dom in the here and now. In fact, a transformed or Spirit-led interior life provides the necessary scaffolding as we move outward to champion an inclusive, beloved community.

The gathering at the Pharisee's house is an example of what *not* to do if we want to embody a different way of doing community. Sure, the guest list included Jesus and a man with edema, but the majority of the guests were folks with religious and societal standing. Their privileged position, in fact, came in full view when they "chose the places of honor" at the table (v. 7). Even the presence of Jesus and the man with abnormal swelling in his body was a political and religious ploy so these privileged people could build up their case against him. It wasn't about fostering an intimate table fellowship at all, but more to do with setting themselves apart so self-righteously from those considered unclean and unorthodox.

As queer folk, we can be and have been subversively different not only in matters of the heart but also in matters of hospitality. Despite being ignored, passed over, disinvited, and barred from sitting at ordinary tables or hosting the eucharistic table, we have remained committed to the call of radical inclusion, to the gathering of all sorts of individuals for *common-union* based solely on grace and love. There

is, indeed, something profoundly "filling" when we
sit around the table just as we are with no intention
except to open our hearts to one another. We call this
gathering a love feast, feasting on the produce of the
earth and on love that knows no boundaries.

Satiated and sustained by a generous helping of
love feast, we turn our attention to the streets and
other spaces of resistance so we can participate in the
ongoing efforts of solidarity and care work with others. We cannot be a one-issue social movement. Our
queerness demands that we form a human chain with
other individuals and communities who, like us, have
been fighting and dismantling structures and systems
of oppression. By virtue of our shared humanity, the
suffering of others touches our own brokenness and
pain, and the healing of others is tied to our willingness to stand next to them in solidarity.[9] This compassionate response is nurtured by a regular practice of
love feasting that also takes the form of listening and
looking deeply into each other's hearts. Here, we rediscover the divinity in each of us, and we come face-to-
face with God in Christ who identified and entered
into our pain and suffering in order to transform it.

This second movement ushers us into the third
act—going upward with the intention to live the
demands of following Christ. The upward and ver-
tical dimension of the religious life can take many
paths. For our purposes, I am suggesting the simple
yet challenging soul habit of contemplative prayer as
a way of supporting and deepening the experience of

discipleship, of becoming like Christ, the messianic host of the banquet. The practice of contemplative prayer is a "prayer of silence and simplicity . . . a deep personal integration in an attentive, watchful listening of the heart. The response to such prayer is not usually one of jubilation or audible witness: it is wordless and total surrender of the heart in silence."[10] Integral to this soul habit is our willingness to shut off the noise of this world and the chatter of our minds so that we can descend interiorly into our heart fully aware of and attentive to the still, small voice of God (Ps. 46:10). This "watchful listening of the heart" is a way of gazing upon the beauty of the Lord (Ps. 27:4), of entering the presence of God with openness and receptivity to claim for ourselves our belovedness and to heed God's call for self-emptying and surrender.[11]

Having been bombarded by vitriol and hate speech for so long because of who we are and whom we love, it is often necessary as a form of defense to talk back and argue for our right to be here. Taking space and claiming our voice is an important part of resisting the evil of oppression, a way of fiercely affirming the divine image in us they try very hard to deface. I wonder, though, if part of keeping ourselves grounded and anchored in love amid the turbulent sea of homo- and transphobic discourse is to bathe our spirit in prayer and our words born in contemplative silence. This might help disentangle us from the psychological scarring that happens when others drag us into the place of shame, and it may free us, or at least get us, to a place where we can pray for those who persecute us. The road to queer discipleship, of imitating Christ, is costly, for it demands that we follow the way of the cross. In fact, in the words of Saint John of the Cross, "Those who take the spiritual seriously should be persuaded that the road leading to God does not require many considerations, methods, or unusual or extraordinary experiences . . . but one thing is necessary—self-denial and self-surrender to suffering and annihilation for Christ's sake. All virtue is contained in this."[12] I take self-denial and surrender to mean not engaging in the same tactics others have used to demean and dehumanize us, not dragging them into the place of shame like what they had done and continue to do to us. I am aware that this is hard, almost supernatural. However, lest we forget, the spirit of Christ is with us; "the spirit of truth which undoes the sacred lie is there to empower us to put up with the hatred which is how the collapsing sacred is held together, and it is by our standing up that the new creation will be brought into being through us."[13] The practice of contemplation, with its focus on mindful beholding of the face of Christ in stillness and adoration, cultivates this heightened awareness of and dependence on the inner work of the Holy Spirit so we can love gratuitously, especially those who consider us not love worthy at all. In fact, we can invite them at the table with the rest of us so together we can all see and taste that Lord is good.

A Queer Banquet

Even before Hannah responded to the call to ministry, they already experienced being welcomed and affirmed in all that they are at a small church in the South. They, with a glim in their eyes, shared this:

> I love my home church. I say all the time that my home church lived into their baptismal vows for me. They nurtured me in my faith, surrounded me with community, and allowed me to grow into this call. I felt especially affirmed by God when this community asked me to help lead and guide our missions work in Appalachia and then asked me to reflect on those experiences in front of the congregation. We also had a group called Rainbow Circle for LGBT Christians, and in that space we would talk about faith, about identity, and what it means to be created in the image of God. Sitting with that group allowed me to grow into my identity both around sexual orientation and in faith and that those two things could be held together in a healthy, beautiful way.

Hannah's story is akin to their receiving an invitation not only to attend a banquet but to be Christ's cohost in welcoming and honoring those in attendance.

And knowing Hannah, I am pretty sure the banquet table will be filled with the choicest of food, wines, and desserts plus a steady flow of joy, laughter, warmth, poetry, dancing, and karaoke singing.

So, the invitation to the eschatological banquet has gone out. Be sure to RSVP and dress up to the theme or category: Do You.

CHAPTER 3

THE QUEERDOM OF GOD

The Parable of the Mustard Seed

Mark 4:30–32

> He also said, "With what can we compare the kingdom of God, or what parable will we use for it? It is like a mustard seed, which, when sown upon the ground, is the smallest of all the seeds on earth; yet when it is sown it grows up and becomes the greatest of all shrubs and puts forth large branches, so that the birds of the air can make nests in its shade."

The faith of queer folk has long been suspected, rejected, and belittled by so many who call themselves defenders of the Christian faith. Yet despite—or because of—this, queer Christians have remained steadfast in their faith,

*which, like a mustard seed, has grown and continues to
provide shelter and inspiration to others on the journey.*

Go Big

Everybody loves a success story, especially those with
a narrative arc that starts small and ends big. Whether
it's *Rocky* or *The Karate Kid*, films like this make a for-
tune at the box office. A good rags-to-riches story will
put a book on the best-sellers list as well. We even brag
about people we know who experienced scarcity early
in life and now live in abundance. There is something
about this contrast and progression, whether reel or
real, that evokes inspiration, hope, and drive within
us—that can-do attitude—that we cannot simply
ignore. We are drawn to it. We imagine ourselves being
in it. We want to be it.

The church loves a success story too. We like to
tell a story that begins with a few believers meeting
in someone's basement, garage, or living room. Over
time, the group grows into a large congregation that
meets at various satellite churches to accommo-
date the increasing number of seekers and longtime
members. What started out as a gathering in the
basement now has a sprawling "basement" for park-
ing and square footage that rivals concert halls and
sport arenas; we call them *megachurches*. The formula
for church growth has been emulated, their pastors
have become sought-after speakers, and their brands
are recognizable not only domestically but across

continents. Many dream about being a part of such a story. Many try to replicate it. Some of us may already be a part of one.

For many Christians, faith is the mover, the unseen force that makes it possible to shift from starting small and ending big, from being ordinary and unknown to achieving significance, even greatness. For many, such success is true faith in action: a faith that can do the impossible, a faith anchored in a God who makes a way when there seems to be no way. This general notion of success offers an experience so strong that it has the potential of filling the void created by moments of doubt and unbelief, pulling people back to a renewal of faith.

The parable of the mustard seed is most often read with an interpretive slant that centers the "miraculous growth of the kingdom, whether in one's heart, in the church, or in society."[1] All we have to do is put our faith and confidence in God, who promises success especially amid life's many twists and turns.

• • •

As much as this is a familiar (and rewarding) reading of the text, a queer reading of the parable takes a different route, moving away from "small becoming big" into something that makes the familiar strange and disrupts the arc of the story to make room for the unexpected. Might there be something about the mustard seed—being the "smallest of all the seeds . . . yet when it is sown it grows up and becomes the greatest of all shrubs [or "trees," as translated in *The Message* or the English Standard Version], and puts forth large branches, so that birds can make nests in its shade" (Mark 4:30–32)—that both reveal and conceal something peculiar about the workings of the divine, about God's work in and through queer lives?

Let's start with some botanical tidbits about mustard seeds. To begin, mustard seeds, though proverbially known for their small size, are not the smallest seeds; orchid and cypress seeds are smaller.[2] Black mustard, which scholars presume is what Jesus was talking about, can grow into a bush that is eight to ten feet tall, but it is not cultivated.[3] It "grows entirely wild, though it is improved by being transplanted; but on the other hand when it has once been sown it is scarcely possible to get the place free of it, as the seed when it falls germinate at once."[4] Based on these descriptions, it seems Jesus was on to something when he used the imagery of the mustard seed that is more subversive than a success story. When we zero in on the symbolic meanings of mustard, trees or shrubs, branches, and birds, we find a doorway into alternate commentaries that are more subversive, twisted, and edgier—*queerky*, if you will.

The inspiration behind this interpretive move is that Jesus, through the parable, has created a "light-hearted burlesque" that parodies the power of the empire, of the big success story: it is the mustard seed—a roadside weed—and not the mighty cedar

(Ezek. 17:22–24) that offers shelter and shade to the beasts and birds of the earth.

> The Kingdom as Jesus sees it break-ing in will arrive in disenchanting and disarming form: not the mighty cedar astride the lofty mountain height but as a lowly garden herb. The Kingdom is asserted with comic relief: what it is and what it will do, it will be and do, appearances to the contrary with-standing. It will erupt out of the power of weakness and refuse to perpetuate itself by the weakness of power.[5]

This would be hard for the mighty cedars of the world to hear, especially those who claim to be the manifestation of divine presence on earth. Who would argue with numbers, influence, power, resources, and reach as key indicators of success?

The sacred, subversive canopy "that is the little mustard seed" only gets more expansive, reaching far corners of the world and providing not only shade and shelter but also a sense of belonging—a place within the divine plan. The burgeoning black mustard bushes are tangible proof that the small mustard seed really does sprout into something big, but not the success of empire.

But we know—and by "we," I mean those of us who have been made to "submit to the cross and the sword"—the mighty cedars: that version of bigness that feeds on the exclusion or elimination of our (fluid and evolving) identity as persons and communities purveys an oppressive brand of holiness or religious piety. Our psyche has been colonized in its core, our mind inhabited by colonizers (usually white, Western, and male), and our spirit crushed into submission so we could become their replicas, breathing ventriloquists of a worldview that aims to dominate and subjugate the othered or the subaltern. They have manufactured people in their own image, all the while sanctioning such missionary work as divinely inspired or God ordained. For their vision to survive, everyone and everything must cohere, support, and propagate this divine brand, with people and institutions firmly planted to carry the work. The mighty cedar, indeed, has grown into a monstrous tree with branches extending everywhere.

Nowhere is this more evident than the branch of cis/heterosexism that continues to draw support and sustenance from the trunk of the mighty cedar of coloniality and empire. But as the parable goes, it's the lowly mustard seed—the roadside weed, the queer folk—that will bring the mighty tree low for those who truly manifest God's reign: God's *queerdom*.

The Queerdom of God

The reign of God is present among us queer folk: a kindom, a queerdom. God's divine work in and through us, like the mustard seed, is small and undetectable, "disenchanting and disarming."[6]

Though the divinity in us is often demonized to protect the stronghold of the mighty (whitey) and patriarchal cedar, the seed of the divine is deeply implanted in us. We are the beloved queers of God, created in the image of the queer God; we are sacred icons just like everyone else, a portal into a different way of being in the world and with each other, a window into the ever-expanding and spacious, gratuitous, transforming love of God that shelters all.

Disenchanting the illusion of might as right and disarming the weaponry of masculinity, the queerdom of God "is not a towering empire, but an unpretentious venture of faith."[7] If one thing is true about the queer faith, it is that it is never pretentious. We are not building an institution; we are cultivating relationship. And despite having our faith demolished, diminished, and demonized, queer folk remain steadfast in letting our little mustard seed grow.

Ziggy, an ordained United Methodist clergy, put his unpretentious faith in full display when he reflected on the result of the United Methodist Church Special General Conference in 2019.

> We all have the same baptism. No one is better than me in the eyes of God. We are all children of God. What gives anyone the right to legislate how God's grace is dispensed? I will always

remember my baptism. I am thankful
for the promise that God will love me,
take care of me, accept me, honor me,
and raise me up. God has not changed
this covenant with me at my baptism.
If they change this covenant, that is on
them. My covenant with God does not
change. I am still who I am. I am still
loved by God; I am a child of God no
matter what they say.

The church, at least Ziggy's denomination, remains
perched on the branch of this mighty cedar. As a case
in point, the calculated triumph of the traditional plan
at the UMC Conference tightened the denomination's
grip on its doctrines and policies regarding the treatment of self-avowed practicing homosexuals. Seeking
unanimity of 438 delegates meant displacing and dis-
membering a significant number of faithful followers
of Christ whose sexuality and gender identity do not fit
the privilege and protection of the traditional cis/het-
erosexual norm.

Like Ziggy, who continues to dedicate his life, labor,
and love to his advocacy and organizing work at Reconciling Ministries Network (RMN), squads of queer
siblings remain undeterred by the outright display of
gender and body surveillance. They have strengthened
their resolve to exercise their sacred call in the face
of the challenges; obstructions; and blatant discrimi-
natory, harmful, and traumatizing practices that have
been and will continue to be deployed against them.

This unpretentious adventure of faith that queer folk try to live out, come hell or high water, is a mark of the presence of God's queerdom in our midst. It is unrelenting, tenacious, and unyielding. The mustard seed—conceived both as a metaphor for God's reign and for an active faith in the queer God—is not and will not be intimidated by the posturing of the mighty cedars of power and privilege. The tenacity of queer faith relies not on numbers or appearances or even growth, but in the hope that the proud will be brought low and the low brought high, and in the belief that Jesus "did not choose the proud cedar but rather the humble mustard in order to express this hope," the hope for a new queerdom.[8]

This new queerdom puts the empire of cis/heterosexism on the defense. When, in Luke's version of the parable, the mustard seeds were sown in the garden, they grew side by side with other plants. Likewise, we may not be as numerous as our counterparts, but we are everywhere. The presence of queer bodies among predominantly cisgender heterosexual bodies that inhabit these religious spaces evokes discomfort, dis-ease, and disorientation. Something about our queerness threatens the norm to its core. That is, the presence of queer bodies in these spaces challenges the conception and experience of their own sexuality as the only and "right" way of embodying one's erotic desires. Couple that with queer folk serving as portals and icons of God and the whole tree is shaken to its core. With fear now running through the veins of that mighty cedar that is cis/heterosexism, they double down on their claim and discourse by rendering queer folk's "humanity—our thoughts, feelings, desires, and longings, not just about our sexuality, but everything that constitutes our personhood—suspect, defective, and unacceptable."[9]

Hence, our bodies are in constant collision with these normative bodies, leaving some, if not most of us, dismembered in all sorts of ways. They have uprooted and thrown us out, but the sower keeps sowing these lowly mustard seeds everywhere, so it is "scarcely possible to get the place free of it," and we keep sprouting in both familiar and unlikely, unexpected gardens and fields and grounds because that is just the nature of the queerdom of God and the queer faith that takes shelter in it. With the apostle Paul, we can say with such conviction that

> we have this treasure in jars of clay to show that this all-surpassing power is from God and not from us. We are hard pressed on every side, but not crushed; perplexed, but not in despair; persecuted, but not abandoned; struck down, but not destroyed. We always carry around in our body the death of Jesus, so that the life of Jesus may also be revealed in our body. (2 Cor. 4:7–10, NIV)

As the parable goes in Mark's version, the queer-dom of God is like a mustard seed that "grows and becomes the greatest of all shrubs, and puts forth large branches, so that the birds of the air can make nests in its shade" (Mark 4:32). The "lighthearted burlesque" that both reveals and conceals the inner workings of the divine is contained in this last verse. First, mustard seeds grow into a shrub, not a tree. But the use of the tree with big branches (at least in some translations) has more to do with a divine logic that usually challenges, interrogates, and humbles human logic. The growth of the queerdom first and foremost is a divine effort, with queer folk and those considered small, insignificant, despised, sinners, and outcasts playing an important role. Second, the growth of this little mustard seed conceals the hidden divine dynamics responsible for its miraculous transformation. Even if hidden, unnoticed, or ignored, the full revelation and benefits of the queerdom of God will come in God's own terms and timing.[10]

But the miraculous growth of this lowly seed from small to big is not the point of the parable. The mustard shrub or tree "is not admired and praised for its own sake but rather as it serves others."[11] That's the punchline—the ultimate message of this parable. The mustard, the smallest of all seeds, turns into the greatest of all shrubs with "large branches, so that the birds of the air can make nests in its shade" (Mark 4:32). In other words, the miraculous growth exists not for its own sake but for the sake of others.

The nesting of "birds of the air" in the branches or in the shade is a common motif that appears in Daniel 4, Ezekiel 17, and Ezekiel 31, which associate birds and trees with fallen empires.

> Drawing on the ancient oriental motif of the world tree, each one is about an image for kingdom and sovereignty; in Ezekiel 17:1–24 it is the King of Israel, in Ezekiel 31:1–18 the Pharaoh, in Daniel 4:1–34 the Babylonian ruler. In each case, however, the image is linked to the prediction of humiliation and downfall, which are interpreted as the consequences of royal arrogance and abuse of power. Only after the falling of the old tree will a new beginning be possible in that a new tree will grow out of a branch in which all birds can live.[12]

At times the mighty cedar of cis/heterosexism feels overpowering, unmovable, and imposing. The arrogance and abuse of power run rampant, and the wounds left behind are deep and excruciating. Yet the queerdom of God remains unperturbed, and its divine work continues with queer folk taking an active role in growing this "new tree" to provide shelter and shade for all. This new tree comes in the form of a beloved community constituted by queer folk and those otherized and subjugated by the dominant group, who are proudly perched in the branches of the old and crumbling tree.

• • •

Being unhoused is a familiar experience among queer folk. Without shelter or shade, most of us, especially queer youth, had to endure abandonment from family and assault, violence, and even death on the streets. Recent studies show that queer youth and young adults have a 120 percent higher risk of experiencing homelessness—often due to family rejection or discrimination because of their gender identity or sexual orientation.[13] The risk is even higher among Black queer youth, who are subjected to vectors of oppression because of their intersectional identities.

To mitigate this, queer folk have found a way to create a home for themselves, or they have been offered a home by their now chosen family. The formation of this new beloved community is fraught with challenges and opportunities because we now must find a way to make room for one another so each can dwell in it as we are. Our shared experience of rejection expands our capacity to inhabit the world of another, and through this deep empathy and identification we can offer not just a shade and shelter, but rest and hopefully shalom.

As we accept this gesture of hospitality, we do not have to be someone other than ourselves just so we can become part of this new household of queer faith.

God's queerdom extends to and includes all of us, and it starts right where we are. From this unique place and circumstance, God will fashion and mold us to be the sort of people we are meant to be—"as lovers of God and lovers of all"—without displacing our queerness.[14] For there is no other place God's queerdom would reign than in each of us.

Every time we hold space for each other, every time we offer shade and shelter, we instantiate this new creation, this new way of being together that the queerdom of God has inaugurated in Jesus Christ. That is, we are ushered into this life-changing event by Jesus Christ, who is prior to us, another Other whose only desire is to affirm and not thwart, grow and not stymie, our unique personhood and our potential for flourishing.[15] Christ, who lives in us, is inducting us into a new way of life, which we live by faith in him who loved us and gave himself for us (Gal. 2:20). Simply, the place of shame inhabited by Christ has also become the place where a new vision of humanity is inaugurated, an "alternative vision of what human beings could be or are meant to be."[16] The new creation has come: the old has gone, the new is here, right now in the concreteness of our lives (2 Cor. 5:17).

I am acutely aware that the mighty cedar can dwarf the growing little mustard seed—that is, the larger reality still tries to trample us, uproot us, and throw us into the fire to be burned. Yet we remain hopeful "that the presence and activity of the God of love, who can make us love our neighbors as ourselves, is our hope and the hope of the world—that the God is the secret of our flourishing as persons, cultures, and interdependent inhabitances of a single globe."[17]

This presence and activity, as the parable shows, usually goes unnoticed, even undetected at times. It doesn't have the usual fanfare or noise or large following we expect of the mighty. But the queerdom of God is not about optics or hogging the spotlight. It is not here to gain "likes," to go viral, get millions of subscribers, or make it to the top of trending topics. It might appear small, but it is big when it comes to its intention to provide a shelter and shade for one and all.

Let's host a homecoming for everyone with the theme or category: Small but Terrible.

CHAPTER 4

QUEER JOY

The Parable of the Hidden Treasure

Matthew 13:44

The kingdom of heaven is like treasure hidden in a field, which [someone] found and reburied; then in his joy he goes and sells all that he has and buys that field.

This chapter describes in detail the experience of joy evoked by the discovery of the queerdom of God. This joy—better yet, queer joy—makes a demand on us to drop all so we gain all.

Finders Keepers

What do the movies *Indiana Jones, National Treasure, Pirates of the Caribbean, Blood Diamond, The*

Mummy, and *Uncharted* have in common? Treasure hunting. There is something exhilarating seeing men (usually white men, which is very telling in itself) go on an adventure in search of religious relics and cultural treasures—things of great value. They go to great lengths just so they can get their hands on (and fill their pockets with) these treasures, whatever the cost. And what joy and pride of accomplishment they express when the treasures are finally found.

The parable of the hidden treasure follows the same theme of joy in finding, as well as the cost of the effort in securing them. Yet the parable offers more when read with queer eyes. In the first line we encounter the use of the word *treasure* as a metaphor for describing the nature and character of the queerdom of God.

The kingdom of heaven is like treasure hidden in a field. When a man found it, he hid it again, and then in his joy went and sold all he had and bought that field.

The word *treasure* is not uncommon. It is the same word that is used as a descriptive stand-in for Christ, the Bible, heaven, or various virtues such as wisdom.[1] The treasure is hidden in a field, not on full display to be seen everywhere or given away to whoever fancies it. It has to be found, and that requires effort. In fact, the treasure in the parable is not merely a thing of great value. It makes a claim on the one who finds it: it drives the person to engage in an elaborate scheme to possess it. The man who discovers the treasure hides it again and, overcome with joy, sells everything to buy the entire field.

But the parable raises ethical questions about how the man finds the treasure. In buying the field, the finder does not reveal his great discovery to the owner; hence, we as readers are left with a moral conundrum. If we are willing to overlook this nuance, the parable can still be about risking all and finding joy. But if what he did was illegal, how do we reconcile the relationship between ill-gotten wealth and the queerdom of God?

Some interpreters consider the finder's actions immoral, and their interpretation of the parable is about the abandonment of all goods and morals.[2] Others consider the action moral and legal on the basis of rabbinic regulations about finding and "lifting—that is, the owner had not lifted the treasure or take possession of it, and therefore did not own it."[3] But focusing on the finer detail of the parable may pull us away from what other scholars consider to be the parable's main point: "When that great joy, surpassing all measure, seizes a man [sic], it carries him away, penetrates his inmost being, subjugates his mind."[4] The affective register of joy that overtakes the man has been described as the "narcissism of finding a lost object . . . an occurrence that breaks expectations and interrupts the everyday." In other words, the overwhelming burst of happiness, excitement, pleasure, exhilaration, and surprise is induced by the unexpected, undeserved, and unearned discovery of something incredibly valuable that could potentially change his life course. The queerdom of God that can upend worldly king-doms lies below the surface like the treasure, waiting to be discovered, to be found. The question is not who owns it. It is "given *before* we know whether the man [*sic*] deserves it. . . . It comes before our deeds."[5] To make this joy complete, one has to drop all to gain all.

Kill/Joy

For queer folk, the discovery of the queerdom of God has evoked myriad affects and effects. Like the finder of the treasure in the parable, I remember being gripped by this inner witness of God loving me as I am. I was captured by the grace of God's investments and interests in and God's deep desires for our individual and collective flourishing that ushers us into a differ-ent realm of possibilities—a future and a world where compassion, justice, and peace reign.

Often, though, it is hard to sift through or discern whether the treasure is genuine and true (the liberative gospel of Christ) or a knockoff (a dubious copy of the message). Still, amid the confusion, the abiding sense of God's accompaniment, participation, and invitation to cocreate this world otherwise remains. But I sus-pect that when we come face-to-face with the genuine and true—that is, the discovery of God's commitment to this ongoing liberation of all God's people and cre-ation—this treasure draws us further and deeper into the wellspring of joy. This reservoir of living water has the capacity to drench the parched soil of legalism and the system of dominating and subjugating hierarchy and privilege that seem so pervasive in the Christian landscape, especially nowadays.

Joy, at least the way I have experienced it, is more than just a feeling. Besides the sense of pleasure, happiness, delight, exhilaration, buoyancy, and lightness, there is also that feeling of a dopamine rush, the bodily gestures of glee: jumping, hands outstretched to share the feeling with others, and even tears. It is a whole-body experience. But there is another dimension beyond the realm of theology that is worth naming, if only to deepen our understanding of this positive human experience, and we can infer it from the man's response to finding the treasure in the parable.

Joy, as an emotion, also includes "how an individual perceives a situation and concern or the individual's evaluation of the situation."[6] Surprised by finding the treasure buried in a field, the man might have experienced a flood of thoughts and ideas—from how the find might bring about significant change in his life to thinking how lucky he might be for discovering it, or from wondering if the owner of the field was aware of the treasure buried to what he could do to secure it for himself. With excitement, delight, and happiness coursing through his veins and with the understanding of this unexpected turn of events, the man appraised the situation to figure out what to do next and acted hastily—he hid it again and then, in his joy, sold all he had and bought that field. Simply, the experience of joy involves an intricate choreography of feelings, thoughts, and behavioral responses overcoming, compelling, and propelling the person to action. Further, from the perspective of positive psychology, the "joyful" person is curious and open to new ways of thinking and being, which the finder of the treasure seemed to have displayed.[7]

Though queer folk have access to and have experienced wellsprings of joy, attempts that obstruct this positive affect from our lived experience are ongoing, relentless, structural, and well-orchestrated. They increase and intensify the negative affect of disgust and shame and justify the lie, that is, that our sexuality, gender identity, and expression are indicators of our flawed nature, by co-opting the name of the divine. Faced with disgusting objects, people generally experience an arresting combination of physical and behavioral reactions, from changes in breathing and distinct facial expressions to nausea and vomiting.[8] There is a reflexive response of avoidance or withdrawal, of pushing the disgusting objects away both physically and psychologically. These responses are preprogrammed in our bodies—the stomach, the vagus nerve, and the brain stem—to allow for "early detection and avoidance of disgust-threats."[9]

To guarantee an aversive reaction, the normative discourse on homosexuality incessantly trumpets the core message that the queer community is a major threat to people's moral, spiritual, and societal well-being (read: cis/heterosexual society). "We must defend ourselves from the queers" is the battle cry, catapulting us to a place of notoriety, enemies to be subjugated, defeated, and banished. On an experiential level, we know quite well those disgusting looks that are thrown at us every time we show up as our fabulous and authentic selves. Our queerness threatens the unchecked but deeply held cis/heterosexual hegemony. If disgusting looks could kill, we would all be gone. And actually, the look has killed some of our queer siblings, often violently and usually targeting Black and Brown bodies. Both in a literal and metaphorical sense, the "normalized violent collectives of heteronormative, cisgender, White supremacist (and classist) ideologies"[10] has killed (and still is killing) the life and the joy of so many of us.

Another insidious conspiracy to deaden the joy among queer folk is the deployment of shame. If the affect of disgust is what is activated among those who adhere to the normative discourse on homosexuality, the pervasive affect of those who hear this rhetoric of hate is shame. Shame is an "innate attenuator circuit" for positive affect.[11] In other words, shame impedes the experience and expression of positive affects (enjoyment and joy). Worse, it interferes with the simple pleasures of daily life.

The bodily contours of someone who is being shamed or feeling ashamed are obvious: eyes are usually averted and downcast, and the neck and shoulders slump as if wanting to disappear. For most of us the experience is all too familiar. There is something about the experience of shame that reduces our humanity to nothingness. When queer bodies are subjected repeatedly to queer shaming, the excruciating pain extends beyond simply blocking the experience of positive affect. It also interrupts effective and affective communication, limiting our ability to engage and experience intimacy and empathy with others. Hence, the experience of shame is not merely solitary, it is incredibly isolating. It leaves us feeling unloved and unlovable, yielding to experiences of depression, anxiety, homelessness, substance abuse, and worse of all, suicide.

> When God kind of plucked me out of my school counseling career, I was really in a place where I was really angry with the church. I was hurt and harmed by them so much because of my sexuality, and I was ready to leave the church. This was, like, 2012 and I had just married my partner at that time who I have been with for 12 years, and my father had just passed, and a lot of things were changing in my life. I just got hired as a lead counselor at a brand-new high school and was a head softball coach.

Mika, a Black queer United Methodist Church clergyperson, did not wait long to share this painful season in her life. The traces of this journey are clear—lines were drawn early on: heterosexuality was the only acceptable expression of human sexuality; the only acceptable expression of human love was heterosexual love. All nonconforming sexualities, gender identities, and expressions outside of the cis/heteronormative hegemony were considered unnatural and incompatible with Christian faith and living. Strengthened by the emotional boosters of disgust and shame, this negative sex messaging sedimented in Mika's psyche, causing her to doubt her agency and the goodness of her sexuality. Her intersecting identities as a woman, Black, and queer also made her life more precarious and vulnerable to various forms of oppression and discrimination, something she still must fight every single day. Though submerged in this morass of negative affect at that time, the flame of joy in discovering the radical work of God's queerdom keeps her afloat and attuned to God's still, small voice.

Queer Joy

Joy—or to be more precise, queer joy—is a still water that runs deep, unperturbed by the chaos on the surface. This aspect of joy is seldom acknowledged or nourished because the more exuberant expression of joy is what gets noticed most of the time. Serene joy is "quieter and calmer . . . not a withdrawn state, but a state in which one is prepared to engage, should the opportunity arise."[12] I would like to think that this is partly what Mika drew from when she was faced with an opportunity to listen deeply and intently to the lure of God back to her sacred call.

> One day, a female student, six feet tall and of Polynesian and Mexican heritage, walked into my office and asked for my help to get through high school. As a potential softball or basketball player in the future, she and I sat down and worked out a plan for her to graduate so she could play ball. Later that year, she came back to my office not asking for help but to tell me something that changed the course of my life. She said, "Why are you still a counselor? You are good at what you do, and you have done so much for this school, but I don't feel that you are appreciated. I feel like God has somewhere else for you to be." At that time God had also been tugging at my heart, and for a while there I was researching schools. When she left, I closed my door and I cried because I knew this was a God thing.

God, in the form of a six-foot mixed-heritage athlete, visited Mika and, without mincing words, gave voice to what she had been hearing in the background that was faint but no less perceptible or recognizable. She experienced that encounter as harmonizing, unitive, and integrating of her personhood and her relationship with God, which are all phenomenological descriptors of joy.[13] A resonance, a familiar yet quiet movement within, began to bubble up, and she cried because she knew that that visit was "a God thing."

Like the man who found the treasure, Mika had an encounter with the living treasure, the gift giver, the source of all good things (James 1:17) beckoning her to claim it for herself because it was given to her as a gift. This time, her joy was made complete, because she dropped all to gain all. Again, like the finder of the treasure in the parable, Mika wasted no time and, with her wife, moved to Denver to study at a seminary as a way of preparing for and living into the call of teaching, preaching, and leading a church. She left her stable and promising career as a counselor and coach, her relations and community she had built over those many years, and started anew. She mused with glee on her face, saying, "I knew that I was where God had wanted me to be. I visited the school in June and by end of July, everything was all in place—a job, a home, and a new community for the next four years."

The parable of the hidden treasure is short and ends abruptly. It offers no hints on how the man used the treasure he found or what became of him. Curiously, perhaps, it was meant to be this short and open-ended so the hearer could imagine various scenarios. Mika, on the other hand, narrated a story that is still evolving past that encounter with that six-foot figure stand-in for God. She is now the lead pastor of a

growing and diverse community in the Desert South-
west. Her ministry blooming and the community viv-
ified by her unique embodiment and presence as a
shepherd. She, after all, was called a "revival baby" in
her younger years, but it was only in her adult years
that she understood the significance of that moni-
ker. It seems that the treasure Mika has found keeps
on giving—healing her so she could bring her full self
to the ministry and in the process enjoin others to
do the same. She is now living into her "blessed" life,
which is another word for joy, as a proud Black queer
clergywoman.

But we still live under a canopy of ideologies and
oppressive and harmful practices that seek to destroy
and negate queer joy, and Mika's story is no exception.
In fact, she has painfully realized that the "hardest
reality was to understand that extreme progressivism,
like extreme conservatism, can cause the same harm
and trauma. And I have experienced this up close and
personal within progressive circles." This leads to an
urgent question: How might we leverage queer joy to
combat the dark arrows of negative affect that now
come from all sides?

Queer joy is power unleashed and can be a threat
against the unrelenting social and spiritual mechanism of exclusion. Whether expressed excitedly or
serenely, queer joy taunts those who try to kill it, as
if saying, "You can try to steal it, but you can never
exhaust it." For it is not merely a pleasant state when
things are better than expected; it also steers and

infuses creativity, imagination, and affiliation as a ready response to current and future challenges and obstacles. It does not wash away the complications and complex emotions that rise up in our quest for social justice, belonging, and flourishing, but cradles and transforms these emotions into something much more subversive and threatening to the dominant group. Here, we owe our deep gratitude to queer Black joy-ing, the "grand ridiculer creating possibilities for organisms to collaborate, fracture, rock with, and throw shade."[14] Think of RuPaul's *Drag Race*, for example. Though meant to entertain, it also fractures and throws shade at toxic cis/heteronormativity and presents a much grander, inclusive, and fabulous vision of the human—in drag. We need a regular dose of queer Black joy so we can "ridicule queerly" every space we inhabit, even or especially our own so we keep growing and joy-ing.

The road ahead is long and winding. Our queer bodies will grow weary at times, our queer spirit will need to be uplifted, and our queer community depends on each of us showing up and taking and holding space for one another. Hence, we need not only attend to these challenges with curiosity and a compassionate heart, but it would also serve us well to lean into positive emotion as well—such as pleasure of "being-with" those who share the same vision and commitment to worlds otherwise, of excitement and satisfaction over small (and large) victories, pride for the personal and collective work that bears fruit, awe for the human spirit and resilience, and more—these all come with our justice and care work. This is akin to pleasure activism, which combines the basic human need to seek pleasure and the promotion of a life well lived for everyone, which I believe is part of queerdom living. It involves both intention and action to "reclaim our whole, happy, and satisfiable selves from the impacts, delusions, and limitations of oppression and/or supremacy."[15] In the same way, the discovery of the queerdom of God claims us; that is, the joy it produces must also be protected, nourished, and sustained at all costs. Don't let anyone steal your queer joy.

So let's laugh our hearts out when we come together. And when we do, let's unabashedly display the theme or category: Queer Bliss.

CHAPTER 5

Q-CONNECTIONS

The Parable of the Sower

Matthew 13:3–8

And he told them many things in parables, saying: "Listen! A sower went out to sow. And as he sowed, some seeds fell on the path, and the birds came and ate them up. Other seeds fell on rocky ground, where they did not have much soil, and they sprang up quickly, since they had no depth of soil. But when the sun rose, they were scorched, and since they had no root, they withered away. Other seeds fell among thorns, and the thorns grew up and choked them. Other seeds fell on good soil and brought forth grain, some a hundredfold, some sixty, some thirty.

This chapter explores the role of the queer community in the active reception of the Word. As a rich soil, our beloved community creates a habitat for queer flourishing. The task of every queer follower of Christ is to cultivate our inner life—the interior garden of the soul—so our outer life radiates the light of Christ that is in us.

Hallowed Ground

Todd and I walked into Broadway United Methodist Church one Sunday morning, at the invitation of a friend who was at our Latin-flavored family picnic the weekend before. I can still picture that very first time I was back in church. I still tear up just thinking about this. It was like a tidal wave of emotions, and this was in the early 2000s. We were going through this process of starting a family and I walked into this church full of gay people. So, this was twenty years or so ago and there were so few places like that, and we never looked for another church since then. It was like stepping over that threshold from the old age into the new age, from the old ground into the new realm where that intersection meets in the community of God, where God is calling them to be, and it was one of the most profound experiences of my life. My calling comes out of being immersed in that community.

The look on David's face was filled with tenderness and gratitude when he shared this part of his story. Something shifted in him as he tried to retrieve this special fragment of a story he carries around in his heart always. I was deeply moved by what seemed to be the beginning of something profoundly transformational in him akin to planting a seed in fertile ground that would produce a nourishing harvest.

The parable of the sower intimates a similar plot, at least a strand of it in terms of what happens to the seeds that fall on "good soil." But there's more drama to the parable before this feel-good climax. It starts with Jesus traveling from one town to the village, proclaiming the good news of the queerdom of God. Surrounded by a large crowd, Jesus taught in parables, including the one about a farmer who went out to sow his seeds.

The next five verses detail the fate of the seeds that fell on different surfaces. The description is vivid and the outcome amusingly predictable. Seeds that fell along the path were eaten up by birds. Those that ended up in rocky places that did not have much soil showed promise, but it was short-lived. The scorching sun and shallow soil offered little support, and the seeds withered away because they had no roots. The seeds that fell among the thorns choked the plants when they grew. Finally, the seeds found their true match, the right surface: the fertile ground. Those that fell on good soil—well, we know what happens to them. They yield a crop way more than what was sown. Quite a fitting ending to a parable, it seems, until you read the punch line.

Why would a farmer waste those precious seeds by indiscriminately tossing them on surfaces that would not produce a yield? The question has provoked some interesting proposals but no definitive answers. Some say that the sowing preceded the plowing, others claim that plowing preceded sowing, and then others make the claim that plowing was done both before and after the sowing. Another point of debate is the size of the yield and its significance.[1]

Options for interpretating the parable are numerous—from focusing on the sower, the seed, the soil, or the harvest to themes about the end times, holding onto God's promise of abundance despite failures, a reflection on Jesus's ministry and the challenge he faced in his proclamation of the message, and the importance of listening and responding to Jesus's message, to name a few.[2]

These interpretive moves get further complicated when we factor in the harsh and difficult language in Mark 4:10–12 about Jesus using the parables to keep listeners from understanding his meaning, followed by the inclusion of verses from an Isaiah passage that indicates that their heart had already hardened so they couldn't understand the parable anyway. The counterargument is that Jesus's use of parables is not to conceal but to reveal his "prophetic message . . . a warning of what is happening—that judgment is inevitable, that people have not responded and will not—and also a challenge and an invitation for people . . . to hear the word and repent."[3]

Later in the same chapter we read a straightforward explanation of the parable, which is a "meditation about the various hearers of Jesus' proclamation."[4] Generally, parables found in the Hebrew Bible, Jewish or Greek, are accompanied by detailed interpretations to ensure that the core message gets across clearly. That is, parables are meant to underscore or offer two contrasting hearers, those who simply hear them but take no action and those who listen deeply to the message and take seriously, in word and in deed, their life implications.

It is to this last point that I want to queer this parable. I think the active reception of the Word (hearing + practice) is not a solo endeavor. The seed does not grow on its own until it is planted in good soil. In the same way, the hearing of the Word depends on a nourishing community that acts as fertile ground so the message can take root and grow and bear fruit. But that's not all. Equally important is the commitment to cultivate our interior "soil" through specific spiritual practices. Here, we see the importance of synergy between the seed and the soil, between the external fertile ground and a deeply personal life of interiority, which together yield a harvest of personal and social transformation.

The presence of a nurturing beloved community is critical to the flourishing of queer life. But what does it mean for queer folk to be part of the queer community? How does being in community with other queer folk facilitate the flourishing of queer life? What difference do queer spiritual spaces make in the lives of queer folk? As a gesture of mutuality, what might one do to enhance this shared life together with other queer folk in the community? Let's explore these questions.

Q-Connections

Human beings require healthy attachments with others in order to survive and thrive. From an early age, we are poised or even compelled to make contact with another person for "daily sustenance, physical safety, empathic attunement, unconditional love, and positive regard."[5] In its absence, our internal world deteriorates; we feel alone and unworthy, lost and disconnected from the very source of life.

For most queer folk this need for attachment is constantly frustrated or disrupted by those near and dear to us. We have heard horror stories of our queer siblings being driven out of their homes and into the streets, cut off from their family and friends, and severed from key relationships and opportunities that bring a sense of meaning and belonging. Expressing this need at its basic and most rudimentary level is often met with rejection, judgment, and, worse, cruelty and violence. Even in religious spaces (at least those that adhere to conservative views), condemnation toward queer folk abounds, and our desire to fully participate in the religious life of the community is often thwarted.

Where can we meet our need for meaningful connection with others that is so critical to our own survival and flourishing? We look for people of our kind and who are kind toward us—the LGBTQIA+ (queer) community. Within this community, proximity fills the gap of forced isolation, safety offers freedom to live authentically, displays of intimacy support bodily integrity, and communal support allows us to live our lives fully. These are like essential plant nutrients that act as a habitat for seeds to grow and bear fruit. In other words, the queer community, as our chosen family, fulfills what has been denied by our biological family and those closest to us.

David's story is a testament to the power of community in birthing his sense of belovedness. He felt seen, noticed, and in the company of those who love and like him as he is. As he said himself, he stepped "over that threshold from the old age into the new age, from the old ground into the new realm where that intersection meets in the community of God." Perhaps he had only heard of this as a promise in the distant future, something to look forward to and move toward, and not something given to him as a gift in the present moment. The new creation that God initiated in Jesus had come upon him, directly and personally, in the presence of a community that had become the embodiment of the reign of God on earth that very day.

The queer community, at its fundamental expression, provides contact with other queer-identifying individuals and our allies—from physical to psychological, from spiritual and sociopolitical relatedness. Being near or close to other queer bodies is a way of experiencing existential validation—that we are seen, noticed, and regarded as another human being. Without the usual prying and judging eyes that litter the heterosexual world, proximity with others fills the gap of forced isolation and loneliness.

Safety is another nutrient that supports growth. Physical safety is paramount to the queer community, given the unremitting assault on and murder of queer bodies. When queer folk inhabit queer spaces, we find comfort and relaxation, markedly different from other spaces where we are always on high alert. Safety is not only the absence of violence but relates to "broader societal acceptances . . . of the possibilities to enacting LGBT identities in taken for granted, indeed ordinary ways."[6]

Related to this is the expression of intimacy that is not only permitted but expected, encouraged, and affirmed in these queer spaces. Displays of affection—from holding hands to giving each other hugs and kisses in public—contribute to a profound sense of wellness and connection with others. In fact, the physical expression of intimacy touches not only the surface of our bodies but triggers a release of oxyto-cin, or the "chemicals of care," that produce sensations of lightness and delight and forges meaningful bonds.[7] Being in community is strongly connected to these practices of intimacy, and for many, "forms of LGBT community or space were understood as such because of the way they supported LGBT+ people safely enact-ing practices of intimacy."[8] It is disheartening to real-ize, though, that the soil of the larger world stifles queer bodies to ensure the curtailment of displays of intimacy in public spaces. Creating and sustaining queer-friendly spaces is all the more urgent if only for the survival of our queer folk.

The queer community is a gathering of individuals with intersecting identities that deepens our apprecia-tion for our differences and expands our opportunities for solidarity. Pride events make this most visible. The celebratory atmosphere of colors, gender identities and expressions, sexualities, shows of affection and belonging, and allyship make manifest exultant pride in being queer. But there is another layer to pride that is quite compelling: queer folk taking over the streets as a way of claiming their queer existence in the pub-lic square. It is indeed a form of resistance against the border created by a cis/heterosexist world, a rec-lamation of physical space that is ours to inhabit just like anyone else. Pride is a political statement, a brave declaration of our right to exist and flourish. There is, of course, a side to these spaces that the community needs to be vigilant about if it is to continue the work of justice making. We need to queer these spaces constantly so that they don't become sites of discrimination and exclusion.[9] Queer relationships and intimate encounters are shaped quite strongly by these intersecting identities, and like most social spaces, we too can be or have been complicit in stoking experiences of ageism, biphobia, classism, dis(ableism), racism, and transphobia within our own community.[10] We must, for our own good and well-being, be each other's support and champion.

Queer Spiritual Spaces

For spiritually and religiously oriented queer folk, occupying sacred spaces is both an act of resistance against the boundaries drawn by the cis/hetero patriarchy and a response to the abiding sense of the transcendent. Spaces, particularly those considered spiritual or sacred, are not merely things to be inhabited. They are not empty spaces to be filled in; instead, they are already configured and constituted by the kind of theology and practices the dominant group deemed correct, spiritual, and godly, to which everyone must adhere or follow.[11] Take the punitive and harmful theology and polity of the United Methodist Church toward queer clergy, as an example. For the longest time, the altar has been manned (pun intended) mostly by the dominant group, white heterosexual men (WHM). They are protective of the space and what it symbolizes for them—the seat of divine power. The performative nature of this carefully choreographed ritual act cements allegiance to cis/heteronormativity in sacred spaces, which in turn bans and banishes those who challenge this religious arrangement. Regular sightings of WHM inhabiting and hogging these spaces on a regular basis make them look natural, expected, and divinely sanctioned.

Queer clergy create disorder that disorients and disrupts the spaces that have been owned and defended by the dominant group. The presence of queer bodies threatens and interrogates their masculinity and their conceptions of God as a straight white male. Related to this, queer theologies that underpin the subversion of these spaces make explicit the very gendered and sexed origin of their own theology. The fervent and passionate display of queer spiritualities challenges their sense of order and control as to how the sacred is experienced and expressed. The response is predictable. They resort to taking control back by banning queer clergy from exercising their gifts and by extension delegitimizing their iconic status as God's beloved.

But queer clergy are not backing down. They take to the streets during Pride, bolstered by a community of other queer siblings and queer allies, and they sashay up with fierceness and confidence to the altar and into the pulpit dispensing their unique gifts and graces without apology. God's beloved queers are on the move, creating "structural disturbance . . . raising insecurities . . . and questioning binaries that serve as normalizing and authenticating structures for a heteronormative way of being" that have kept everyone—men, women, genderqueer, trans, and children of all shapes and colors—chained to their perceived superiority.[12]

Queer folk require this kind of fertile ground for us to continue to hear the gospel of liberation and understand and embody what this means for our lives and those around us. This kind of habitat deepens and expands our roots, so we remain deeply anchored when elements of all kinds threaten to uproot, destroy, or turn rich soil into a wasteland. The nutrients provided by the queer community also strengthen our resolve to not let the principalities and powers—structures of oppression—diminish or question our belovedness, snuff the light within, and deny us our right to call these sacred spaces home.

Interior Garden

The active reception of the gospel message also entails treasuring the word within, letting it take root so our consciousness, our heart's desire, and ways of being "pulsate with the heartbeat of God."[13] A way to tend to this interior work is through the practice of contemplation, which is both a gift of God and a fruit of regular meditation on and reception of the Word of God. God's loving attention is directed toward us always. In response, we ready the ears of our heart and mind so we can hear God and pattern our ways to the ways of Christ in all of life.

Contemplation is a form of listening deeply to the still, small, and gentle voice of God. It is a

> self-forgetting attention, a humble receptiveness, a still and steady gazing, an intense concentration so that emotion, will, and thought are all fused and lost in God who embraces them all. Gradually, by a deeper and deeper process of self-merging, a communion is established between the seer and what is seen, between him [*sic*] and who feels and that which he feels.[14]

In other words, the path of contemplation leads us to an abiding, loving, and experiential knowledge of God not abstractly but concretely shaping and transforming our quotidian queer life.

Some habits of the soul will help sustain our commitment to the spiritual practice of contemplation. They include the habit of the solitude of the heart, which is more than taking time alone to be with God somewhere quiet, though that is an integral part of it. It is about sharpening the "quality of our awareness of our relationship with God with all that lies within, and which gives meaning and purpose."[15] *Lectio divina*, or divine reading, is another path. In *lectio divina* we incline to listen to the Word of God with both attention and a willingness to read it unhurriedly, purposefully, and in anticipation that God will speak to us directly. Another habit is the prayer of silence, which is an active shutting off of the noise and chatter both within and outside of us. This age of surround sound not only drowns our capacity to listen deeply, but also distracts us from experiencing attentiveness and the watchful listening of the heart. A simple way to do this is to set aside about five to ten minutes during the day for mindful breathing as a way of quieting the mind. Praying with icons also cultivates the practice of contemplation. We draw from the Eastern Orthodox tradition, whose use of icons facilitates the deepening of prayer life. This visual representation of the divine or the spiritual life "inspires us to be still, to behold, to gaze upon, to pray, to be fully present with and attentive to what is represented before us."[16]

These are just some of the soul habits that will help cultivate our interior garden so the seed, or the Word of Christ, goes deeper and continues to grow. These habits can also act as a buffer against the birds that will steal queer joy, thorns that will encroach upon queer life, and scorching sun that will try to dry up queer passion.

The rich soil that bears the seed sown also means engaging in the ongoing work of queering texts, theologies, and traditions that have harmed us and transforming them into sources for further resistance and subversion. The work of our queer siblings includes turning texts of terror into texts of love, affirmation, and acceptance through defensive apologetics, reimagining texts, turning theology upside down, and privileging the ethic of love in the reading and the interpretation of these texts.[17] This, of course, generates synergy and collaboration (cross-pollination) with other queer projects that champion equality and rights. The exploration of queer lived experience as the site of knowledge production through social scientific research demonstrates the agency of queer folk as "social actors . . . to transcend, challenge, and subvert religious orthodoxy, and creatively re-contextualize and adapt their faith."[18]

This is akin to producing a crop—a hundred, sixty, or thirty times what was sown (Matt. 13:8). Though much work remains to be done, we can at least enjoy the harvest so graciously poured upon us by our queer ancestors who toiled day and night to ensure daily sustenance, safety, and our significance as queer folk. The fruits of their hard and heart labor bear seeds that we have now been entrusted to sow. And the moment is ripe for queer folk to sow seeds of justice, loving-kindness, and excitement over what God is doing in our midst, with queer folk as the protagonists in this unfolding liberative story. Just like what Jesus said to his disciples (Matt. 9:37–38), "The harvest is plentiful, but the laborers are few; therefore ask the Lord of the harvest to send out laborers into his harvest." Well, that prayer has already been answered.

We are the answer to that prayer, so let's "werk it." And while praying, let us imagine donning ourselves with the theme or category: Queer Fiesta/Carnival.

CHAPTER 6

QUEER BODIES

The Parable of New Wine in Old Wineskins

Luke 5:37–39

No one puts new wine into old wineskins; otherwise, the new wine will burst the skins and will spill out, and the skins will be ruined. But new wine must be put into fresh wineskins. And no one after drinking old wine desires new wine but says, "The old is good."

This is a meditation on what it means for our material, corporeal, queer flesh (new wineskin) to become a vessel for the ongoing liberative purposes of God in Jesus Christ for all of creation (new wine).

The Old and the New

I bought a quilt at a thrift store when I was living in Boston. The block design is rectangular and is patched together in different sizes with different shades of blue and green. I use it primarily as a throw when I read, watch TV, or work on my laptop. It's comfortable, light, and eye catching. Because it has covered me (and the sofa) over many seasons of life, some of the squares needed replacing or repair and some small holes could have used some stitching. Thankfully, my mom knows how to sew, and she worked wonders on that quilt. The only thing is some of the colors and patches used to repair it do not match the hues of the blues and greens in the original. But I'm fine with it; it still brings me comfort and evokes good memories of my life in Boston.

The parable of the new wine in old wineskins comes after the other parable that no one tears a piece of a new garment to patch an old because the patch from the new will not match the old. I chuckled when I started working on the parable of the new wine in old wineskins because that is exactly what we ended up doing with my quilt: we added new patches that didn't match. My mom did not tear up a new garment to do it, but the look of the quilt changed—a tangible version of the parable.

The example of the quilt may be trivial compared to what these two parables are trying to get us to think about, but there is something about mixing the old and the new, especially when it comes to our spiritual journey as queer folk. As we queer the parable, let's start here:

> No one pours new wine into old wine-
> skins; otherwise, the new wine will
> burst the skins and will spill out, and
> the skins will be ruined. But new wine
> must be put into new wineskins. And
> no one after drinking old wine desires
> new wine but says, "The old is good."

Jesus tells the parable in the context of table fellow-ship with some notable people whom he seems to pri-oritize and enjoys hanging out with. This may appear simple, but "Jesus' *practices* at the table, manifest in this scene primarily in his choice of eating companions but also in the depiction of this meal as a festive occasion, are joined with his *teaching* at the table. Both commu-nicate, via deed and word, the nature of his ministry and the concomitant enlargement of the boundaries of God's people."[1] To an extent, Jesus is already embody-ing the meaning of the parables he shared later over the meal. That is, he is incarnating what it means to live into God's expansive and inclusionary grace that does not lead to a rejection of one group and the embrac-ing of another, but calls for repentance and openness to make God's "ancient purposes" come to fruition in Jesus Christ.[2] I interpret God's ancient purposes as

God's steadfast commitment for the liberation and flourishing of all.

This interpretation of the parable counters the prevailing idea that Jesus was distancing himself from the religious leaders of the day by claiming that his new teaching was better than historical Jewish beliefs and practices.[3] By bringing back the theme of enfleshing "God's ancient purposes" as concretely practiced by Jesus Christ with his "table manners," we get a glimpse of what is possible—and preferable—beyond our groupthink tendencies.

If we read the parable backward, that is, trace how the teaching came about, we find that Jesus's parables were a response to the protests being made by the religious elites who had status, power, and privilege. They were critical of his associations with "tax collectors and sinners" (Luke 5:27–33). Their protest doubled down on the social order and boundaries that Jesus was challenging, even dismantling, to open the way for "spiritual and social restoration for these outcasts."[4]

With this as a backdrop, the parable serves as a way to link the practices of Jesus to the ancient story of God's dealing with Israel by drawing on people's everyday knowledge that new wine didn't do well in old wineskins.[5]

Queer Bodies as New Wineskins

Our queer reading of the parable goes further, though still in continuity with the "ancient purposes of God."

Like the tax collectors, we too have been labeled as sinners, and yet in God's eyes, we are vessels worthy of receiving and sharing the new wine. How, then, might our human skin, our corporeal bodies, be prepared to receive and continue to hold the (out)pouring of this new way, the Jesus way of bringing into "fruition the ancient purposes of God"?[6] Put another way, how might our queer bodies be vessels for the ongoing liberative purposes of God in Jesus Christ?

The body. The queer body. The queer body serving as a vessel for the new wine is a strange claim to make. It is strange because within our Christian tradition, generally, the issue of the body—its material and corporeal dimension—receives scant attention or is even deemed irrelevant and threatening to the life of the spirit, except, of course when it is spiritualized (e.g., when talking about the body of Christ or the fleshly incarnation of the Word as God). It is stranger still, and certainly heretical for many, to conceive of the queer body as an anointed vessel of God since the heteronormative discourse on human sexuality that circulates around us marks queer bodies as sacrilegious and never sacred. Only a few will make that bold and strange claim. But lucky for us, the stranger a thing is, the more we tend to bring our queerness to it. And we are going to do just that.

We begin the journey to this unfamiliar territory by attending to the particularity of our body that participates in the unfolding of this new reality. Our first task in this relational dynamic between the vessel and the new wine is to reacquaint ourselves with every part of our body with curiosity and kindness—the sensations we feel, the movements we make, the feelings and thoughts we hold—as a way of preparing to receive and contain the new wine. Our bodies are not empty vessels that wait passively to be filled up, but are willing and active participants in bringing these ancient purposes of God into the present.

As a basic practice of intimately knowing our bodies, we bring our awareness to our material, corporeal selves by doing a gentle scan—starting from the head down to our feet—slowly, gently breathing into them. To deepen this much-needed body work, I invite you to reflect on the following questions.

- What sensations are you picking up as you scan your entire body?

- How do you feel as you do this?

- What thoughts are emerging for you?

If you experience any tightness or pain or pressure, simply breathe through it, cradling it just like a mother, father, or caregiver soothing a child. Practice gentleness toward your body, and be open and present to it with compassion.

It is possible that as we do this general body scan, we will become aware of our queer embodiment—that part of us that says, "I feel, I sense my existence . . . I experience."[7] To deepen this to another level of awareness, I invite you to reflect on the following questions.

- When did you first become aware of your sexual orientation, that you are drawn or oriented toward another person in an erotically charged manner? By this, I mean feelings, thoughts, sensations, bodily reactions, and physical and sexual attraction you have for a particular sex or both sexes.

- What was it like to realize or discover that your body in all its fullness and complexity was responding erotically (and not simply sexually) to someone perhaps of the same sex or gender? How did that make you feel?

- What was it like to have this experience— that is, to feel those feelings (e.g., pleasure, excitement, anxiety, fear, shame), to have those thoughts (e.g., this feels so good yet I feel so bad for having these good feelings about it), to become aware that your body was responding sexually in a certain way to a particular person?

By drawing our attention to our body in this manner, we make a claim that our queerness, broadly conceived, is a bodily event first and foremost. We experience these erotic desires not as abstractions, but as lived experience in and through our physical, material body.

How we make sense of, describe, and represent this experience is often where it gets complicated, especially when we reclaim our queer embodiment as a perfectly imperfect mediator of God's presence in the world. Our queer body is not only a lived and living body, but also an "object for others," where meaning and value are assigned to it (usually degrading, debasing, devaluing); it is "not a thing, it is a situation: it is (my) grasp on the world,"[8] the same way the world grasps us back, often tightly most of the time. It is also "creative and spontaneous, strongly affected by its immediate situation," usually with aftereffects.[9] Our queer embodiment, our lived and experiencing body, is embedded in and profoundly shaped, molded, and influenced by—and to an extent also permeating and affecting—the surrounding world.

Further, our particular body is sexed, gendered, and raced, with physical (dis)ability, belonging to a particular ethnicity, class, culture, and citizenship, perhaps with religious and spiritual sensibilities that together "shape embodied subjectivity in contextually specific ways."[10] The contours of this embodiment occur in and through relations with others and the world and are inextricably linked to relational and often hierarchical power undergirded by regimes of truth or (heteronormative) discourse.[11]

As an example, I describe myself as a cisgendered, queer, Filipino Canadian, able-bodied professional, an unattached man with a deep yearning for the spiritual, embedded in a predominantly white space, watched but not truly seen by a white gaze, and constantly navigating and colliding with the institution of cis/

heterosexuality in myriad ways. These overlapping social identities accentuate the fact that my queer body is not only distinctly corporeal but also social with "crucial political implications."[12]

There is no better way to unpack this more concretely than to sketch out how queer bodies navigate religiously oriented spaces, especially those with conservative leanings and commitments (like the ones inhabited by my interviewees early on in their queer quotidian life). This will also have a bearing on the many ways queer bodies have been denied access and opportunities to become sacred receptacles of the new wine because of the way our embodiment affects how these spaces are configured.

The configuration of space is never neutral. In fact, this social space massively precedes us and is prior to us with its attendant discourses and discursive practices.[13] Put another way, we are born into a world or show up in these spaces already "inhabited, shaped, and made familiar to us by others," which then gives our queer bodies the "capacity to be oriented in this way or in that."[14] For queer folk, that orientation is to be in a "straight" line that institutional cis/heterosexuality has already drawn prior to and for us and that the dominant others already follow.

I remember as a young person being confronted by a church elder to "act straight," that is, to act the conventionally masculine stereotypes or the exact opposite of effeminate mannerisms—strong, stoic, and with a swagger. That this happened just outside of the church immediately after worship proved just how straightly configured and policed this sacred space was. For many years, I have contorted my body to fit this heterosexual mold because acting bent has no place in a straight (religious) world. Soon after my book *God's Beloved Queer* came out, I received few invitations, if any at all, to preach at a church I had attended and served for many years. And there are myriad instances like these that occur with such regularity that regard our queer bodies and queer commitments as falling—and failing—outside of the straight line and therefore unworthy to receive and dispense the "new wine."

This form of body surveillance underscores the "spatiality of sexuality, gender, and race," which dictates how queer bodies inhabit spaces as well as "who or what" we inhabit spaces with, which then makes "certain things, not others available."[15] In the example of my experience, the message is loud and clear; I do not have full access or am not permitted to have access to the divine because of my queer embodiment. In fact, this is precisely what is underneath the United Methodist Church's outright refusal to allow queer clergy full participation in the religious and communal life of the Church. And in a way, the Church serves the institution of cis/heterosexuality to ensure clear demarcation between what is natural, divinely sanctioned, and considered the norm (read: cis/heterosexuality) and what is deviant, demonized, an abomination, and considered incompatible to Christian faith and practice

(read: queer sexuality). The requirement to always follow the straight line originates from and is sustained by
heteronormative discourse that circulates around us.

> By treating heterosexuality as norma-
> tive (heteronormative) or taken for
> granted, we participate in establishing
> heterosexuality—not sexual orienta-
> tion or sexual behavior, but the way it
> is organized, secured, and ritualized—
> as the standard for legitimate and
> prescriptive socio-sexual behavior, as
> though it were fixed in time and space
> and universally occurring.[16]

The power of this discourse, based on my own personal collision with it, is that it is mostly unchecked,
unchallenged, and assumed, and everyone is expected
to follow the "straight line." The elder of the local church
assumed that acting straight was divinely sanctioned,
the pastor I served with for many years assumed that
God-talk is always straight-talk, and the assemblage
at the Special General Conference assumed that the
freedom sought by the queer community within the
denomination is "out of line." Worse, the proliferation
of cis/heteronormativity as it has unfolded in these
spaces (and everywhere else) found its legitimacy by
co-opting the name of the sacred, which then gives it a
quasi-divine status.

The repeated articulation, demand, and expectation to be in a straight line in all ways possible—from the cognitive to affective to behavioral, from intrapsychic or personal to intersubjective to social—is performative through and through. That is, these seemingly mundane occurrences that happen too frequently in myriad spaces are a way of enacting the reality of the straight world with our bodies, making it appear natural and universal, and yet that reality remains a social invention. The cis/heteronormative discourse and discursive practices maintain their power by the continual repetition of gender acts in the most mundane of daily activities.[17]

What happens, then, when queer bodies show up in these "secured, organized, and ritualized" straight spaces? A collision at least on two levels: one intrapsychic and the other relational and social. I believe, as queer folk, that we have an innate sense that our erotic desires are simply part of our physical and bodily makeup. They are as "normal and natural" as any other bodily function or expression. That innate sense is coupled with an inner witness, however faint this may be, that our queerness could be a source of delight, pleasure, and orientation toward another person. All these bodily and psychical manifestations collide against the discourse and practices of heteronormativity that circulate around us, are prior to us, and have already inhabited and shaped our environment. Given its power, influence, reach, and supposedly sacred status, it clashes forcefully against our still developing inner sense and witness of queerness that it often leaves us in a state of confusion, self-doubt, shame, trauma, and despair. The relational-social collision intensifies the impact of heteronormativity on us and more. Where our psychic struggle is internalized, the relational-social collision is public, exclusionary, humiliating, and often fatal; consider our queer siblings who were murdered for simply being themselves. Worse, it is institutionalized, sanctioned, and supported by large numbers of people and communities across the globe. It has the backing of the "bureaucratic state, with its criminal code, police, professional groups, official knowledge, and social policies," as well as religious polity and practices.[18] And this social other, unaffected by our existence, pain, and trauma, is "intricately involved in bringing us into the being"— that sort of person that resembles the "straight world" in some fundamental but soul-sucking ways.

But guess what—and you probably have an inkling about it already. As much as the social order, or configuration, and hierarchy are prior to us, there is another Other that preceded all this and is invested in our own flourishing.

> God is more like nothing at all than like anything that is, because God is not a member of the same universe as anything that is, not in rivalry with anything that is. God is not an object within our ken; we find ourselves as

objects within God's ken. God is massively prior to us, and God's protagonism is hugely more powerful than any possible action or reaction which we might imagine.[19]

As queer folk, we are being invited or ushered into a life-changing event by someone who is prior to all of us, another Other whose desire is only to affirm and not thwart, grow and not stymie our unique personhood and its many possibilities, that the process of new creation and a new way of being together is released through the gratuitous love of the queer God. To put it in the language of this parable, the vinedresser keeps producing new wines, but the old wineskins will not be able to contain this fresh outpouring—that is, God's liberation for all; it will "burst" them. With queer bodies as a vessel of this new wine, adherents of the religiously sanctioned cis/heteronormativity will double their efforts to ensure these vessels do not come near their spaces (or altar), are discarded, and labeled "trash" or to be "recycled" as straight.

Integral for this (human) wineskin to hold the new wine is to listen and lean into that still, small, gentle voice that says, This is my queer child whom I love and am well pleased (Matt. 3:17). Let this voice be the dominant voice as we intentionally and without apology inhabit this world that is mostly inhospitable toward us, like a new wine settling in and expanding the new wineskin. And over time "we become what we hear," so to speak, and really embrace, own, and manifest being truly and madly God's beloved queers. Other practices are worth investing our time in because they position us better to participate in God's ongoing liberative work—from meditation, gardening, dance, and art as self-care, to friendships and solidarity work with others.

I am curious to know what you have been doing to support your flourishing. What impact are you making as you seek to live into God's call into your life? What has helped or might help bring more delight and pleasure into your life? What areas of your life still need the flavor or the taste of and the space for this new wine? How might the queer collective support the "fugitive art of social life—or the acts every life working, studying, talking, plotting, loving, sharing meals, walking with others, consoling, and dancing."[20] Sean, another UMC clergy who took part in this research, embodied this fugitive art when he said,

> I grew up with a very distinct sense of justice related to my identity as a person of color. My dad made sure to instill that in me and in my sister. I am a fourth- or fifth-generation Chinese American, and we are descendants of the very first Chinese in America who were persecuted and suffered—I mean horrendous violence—simply for their race and ethnicity. My ancestors

immigrated before and during the
period of Chinese exclusion, and they
were some of the first illegal immi-
grants in this country. We were farm-
workers doing the backbreaking work
that no one else wanted to do. And so
yes, I have a very intersectional well-
developed sense of justice that I can
really thank my dad for, and I carry that
on today, especially today as we try to
create a more inclusive community
within our denomination.

Whatever it is that you are doing, know that you
are good enough as you are, that the skin you are in
brings pleasure to God who created you and so deli-
cately and wonderfully made you. And as this queer
body expands and flourishes, both personally and com-
munally with others, we help bring about what it truly
means to be the body of Christ, not in abstractions but
in a material, physical, corporeal, and corporate manner. Now, think about that.

In the meantime, bring all the new wine to the
table garbed with theme or category: Queer Body
Power.

CHAPTER 7

QUEER FATHER

The Parable of the Lost Son

Luke 15:11–32

Then Jesus said, "There was a man who had two sons. The younger of them said to his father, 'Father, give me the share of the wealth that will belong to me.' So he divided his assets between them. A few days later the younger son gathered all he had and traveled to a distant country, and there he squandered his wealth in dissolute living. When he had spent everything, a severe famine took place throughout that region, and he began to be in need. So he went and hired himself out to one of the citizens of that region, who sent him to his fields to feed the pigs. He would gladly have filled his stomach with the pods that the pigs

were eating, and no one gave him anything. But when he came to his senses
he said, 'How many of my father's hired
hands have bread enough and to spare,
but here I am dying of hunger! I will get
up and go to my father, and I will say
to him, "Father, I have sinned against
heaven and before you; I am no longer
worthy to be called your son; treat me like
one of your hired hands."' So he set off
and went to his father. But while he was
still far off, his father saw him and was
filled with compassion; he ran and put his
arms around him and kissed him. Then
the son said to him, 'Father, I have sinned
against heaven and before you; I am no
longer worthy to be called your son.' But
the father said to his slaves, 'Quickly,
bring out a robe—the best one—and
put it on him; put a ring on his finger and
sandals on his feet. And get the fatted
calf and kill it, and let us eat and celebrate; for this son of mine was dead and
is alive again; he was lost and is found!'
And they began to celebrate.

"Now his elder son was in the field,
and as he came and approached the
house, he heard music and dancing. He
called one of the slaves and asked what
was going on. He replied, 'Your brother
has come, and your father has killed the
fatted calf, because he has got him back

safe and sound.' Then he became angry and refused to go in. His father came out and began to plead with him. But he answered his father, 'Listen! For all these years I have been working like a slave for you, and I have never disobeyed your command, yet you have never given me even a young goat so that I might celebrate with my friends. But when this son of yours came back, who has devoured your assets with prostitutes, you killed the fatted calf for him!' Then the father said to him, 'Son, you are always with me, and all that is mine is yours. But we had to celebrate and rejoice, because this brother of yours was dead and has come to life; he was lost and has been found.'"

This piece helps us ponder what it means for us to be like the queer father, mother, or parent and to allow this queerness to imbue our ways of being with others so that when the offer of love is rejected or missed, we can still choose to love them no matter what.

Perhaps one of the best known parables in the New Testament, the parable of the lost son, touches the very heart of the human predicament and the extravagant heart of God, which will be our focus. Like the preceding chapters, we will begin by looking at the interpretation of the parable in its immediate context and then queer it, gleaning wisdom relevant to queer life.

Luke 15 contains the "Lost Trilogy"—the parable of the lost sheep (vv. 1–7), the parable of the lost coin (vv. 8–10), and the parable of the prodigal (or lost) son (vv. 11–32). All of the stories were told to a mixed audience of "tax collectors and sinners . . . and Pharisees and teachers of the law." The religious leaders raised their eyebrows about Jesus's affiliation with the sinners. Our parable, the last of the trilogy, describes an intimate family dynamic so familiar it feels as if our own story is being told—a story that runs the gamut from love rejected to love offered amid expected and often repeated rejection.

Love Rejected

The parable starts with an impudent request by the younger son to his father: "Father, give me the share of the wealth that will belong to me." The gravity of such a brazen self-assertion might elude us unless we are familiar with the Middle Eastern culture. In this context asking for one's inheritance while the father is still alive is tantamount to wishing him dead.[1] The son's urgency to satisfy his earthly desires and his drive for independence far outweighed his emotional ties, the proximity to his father, and earthly provisions that had always been available to him. He wanted nothing of this sort, as the parable indicates, except to get everything he could for his own gain.

The response of the father is equally as outrageous in its quietness and overflowing generosity: "So he divided his assets between them." The depth of the father's love for his son is not how a Middle Eastern patriarch would have responded. Ordinarily, such a shameless request would be met with an angry refusal, especially because there is no "law or custom among the Jews or Arabs which entitles the son to a share of the father's wealth while the father is still alive."[2] Not only did the young man wish his father dead, but he also defied cultural laws and mores without blinking an eye. Despite all these transgressions, the father remained gracious and forgiving, a gift he offered both of his lost sons.

What happens next is predictably tragic—it is like watching a train wreck, and you can't look away. The entire village is a witness to this unfolding drama perhaps feeling all the feels that go unnamed in the parable—shock, horror, anger, disbelief, shame, and sadness. In haste, the younger son put his inheritance up for sale and by extension, publicly shamed his father who was still in good health, very much alive, and living in the same village.[3]

He went off to a distant country, a place where no one knew him or his story, a place where he could be anybody, bereft of any relations or form of account-ability. With oodles of resources at his disposal, he lived without restraint, caving in to his every whim. He not only squandered his wealth in wild living, he also squandered his life,[4] his family's life, that had cra-dled, raised, protected, and provided for him.

After blowing his abundance, the worst form of scarcity visited him: "a severe famine took place throughout that region, and he began to be in need." Being a stranger in a strange land, he had no one and nowhere to turn to. The logical next step, of course, was to return home. Perhaps, but this was not always the case in the Middle Eastern cultural milieu governed by a social code of honor and shame.[5] The moment the son returned home he would be subjecting himself to public shame, the same way he subjected his family when he took off in haste with his father's coffers.

To save face (or his pride), "he went and hired himself out to one of the citizens of that region." Desperate times call for desperate measures. He "glued himself" to a Gentile man who owned a herd of pigs and therefore had food.[6] The son demonstrated the same behavior he showed toward his father, and for the same reason: for self-gain in the form of survival. The parallelism goes even further:

> The son sought to rid himself of very easy service to his father and ended up offering very difficult service to a foreigner. . . . The result of his lostness was that he exchanged living in his father's palace for living in the wilderness, and the companionship of his family for the companionship of pigs,

and the good food of that palace for
karobs, and plenty for famine.[7]

His dire condition was accentuated by his longing
to "[fill] his stomach with the pods that the pigs were
eating, and no one gave him anything." The pigs had
been feeding off of pods, and he had nothing. This
reversal of affairs led him to play his last card in a
manner reminiscent of what we would call a self–pep
talk. It is quite convincing if we simply peer into this
internal conversation and behavioral rehearsal that has
often been interpreted as an act of repentance on his
part.

> When he came to his senses, he said,
> "How many of my father's hired ser-
> vants have bread enough to spare, but
> here I am dying of hunger! I will get
> up and go to my father, and I will say
> to him, 'Father, I have sinned against
> heaven and before you. I am no longer
> worthy to be called your son; treat me
> like one of your hired hands.'" So he set
> off and went to his father. (vv. 17–20)

Repentance as a sudden realization of wrongdoing
followed by an actual expression of remorse and restoration of broken relationship is indeed intimated in
this section of the parable, and traditionally, this has
been the call to action for those who identify with the

prodigal son and his change of heart (which really is all of us to varying degrees). For most, if not all of us, turning away from the old and into the new has indeed brought us back into the arms of the divine. Indeed, when it comes to this parable, the message of reconciliation with God is self-evident.

But there is another queer way of interpreting the story, especially in the context of the preceding two parables. As in the parables of the lost sheep and the lost coin, the parable of the lost son drives home the point of "repentance as acceptance of being found."[8] In a way this shifts the focus away from centrality of the lost sheep, coin, and son and the spotlight turned onto the finders—the shepherd, the woman, and the father. In other words, the protagonists in these parables are those who seek to find the lost.

Of course, this is not always obvious to the reader, especially when the words used in subsequent verses are loaded terms and phrases like, "arise," "go to my father," "I have sinned against heaven and before you," and "I am not worthy to be called your son." In fact, these are the stuff of altar calls, hymns, and sermons that declare that something deeply spiritual or transformational has occurred.

But a close reading of these verses reveals a familiar gesture the younger son has been signaling. His rehearsal and display of repentance camouflage his proclivity for self-assertion. And he does it subtly, first by declaring that he is no longer worthy to be called his son and then by asking to be a hired servant. Sounds reasonable, right? After all, he is trying to put his best foot forward in humility.

However, things are not what they seem.

A supposedly repentant son dictates the terms of his relationship with his father, just as he did at the beginning of the parable. Not only was he taking the lead in the father-son dynamic yet again, but he was also trying to prove that he could become worthy of being his father's son again. His confession, "I am no longer worthy to be called your son" is rendered in other translation as "I am not *now* worthy to be called your son." In his mind, it was just a matter of time before he could earn his sonship back. Once again, he was "looking out for number one, namely, himself."[9]

When he went to his father, all his planning (or scheming) was met with an absence of any sort of let's-work-through-this conversation; instead he faced an outrageous display of compassion, grace, and loving mercy at the hands of his queer father.

But before we delve into the queerness of the father, let's look at the other lost son, the older brother.

Love Missed

The older son was no different from his younger brother in terms of how he understood his relationship with his father. His is love missed, stunted, and driven solely by obligation. It is still a form of rejection but in a more controlled and calculated way—until, of course, it bursts open with anger and resentment spilling everywhere.

Like his younger sibling, he too came from the field, but he missed the dramatic reunion between his father and his brother. The journey back to the house from the field symbolizes the relational distance he felt from his father. And it took a happy reunion complete with music, dancing, and feasting for him to unleash his bottled-up emotions.

While the entire village was living it up in joyful celebration, the older son stood near the house, bewildered by all the fanfare. Instead of going inside to check it out and perhaps join the party, he chose to remain outside and relied on one of their servants to fill him in. The servant gave him the news: "Your brother has come, and your father has killed the fatted calf because he has got him back safe and sound."

That was the last straw. What had been simmering underneath found its way to the surface, causing him to blow up in anger. He also refused to go in, which was an act of dismissal and defiance against his father's attempt to rebuild their household.

Despite all that, the father extended the same level of care and attention to his older son. Instead of charging toward him, "he came out and began to plead with him" to celebrate his brother's return. Described more vividly, "The father, in very painful self-emptying love, leaves the seated guests and proceeds to the courtyard . . . searching for him," perhaps searching for another lost son.[10]

The son remained unconvinced and launched into a litany of complaints and judgments. First, he started by omitting the honorific "Father" and instead, with disdain, uttered, "Listen!" as if talking to an inferior. Second, he made claims about himself that were so self-righteous that he became the aggrieved party by profiling himself as a slave to his father, as an upright person who never disobeyed orders, and as the one deserving of restitution. In other words, he saw himself as the "good son" who was treated badly because his father played favorites. Worse, he made all of these accusations in the courtyard to shame his father and to steal the spotlight away from his restored brother. Like his younger sibling, his self-righteous behavior and red-hot tirade were met with a douse of gentle spring coming from the nonreactive, merciful, and compassionate touch of his (queer) father.

Love, No Matter What

Love that is rejected and love that is missed are countered by the father's love, no matter what. It is queer through and through. Let me count the ways.

The queer father, transcending the Middle Eastern patriarchal norm, did not retaliate and punish his younger son, who had wished him dead by asking for his inheritance. Instead, he "divided his assets between them," no questions asked. The father simply granted the son's request not only for the "immediate possession of what would normally have come to him only at the death of his father," but also for self-determination free from his father's love.[11] Perhaps, with deep sorrow, he willingly submitted himself to "enduring the agony of rejected love and granted his request for freedom to reject the offered relationships."[12]

A Short Interlude

How many times have we made the same gesture of self-assertion toward God, leaving behind our "spiritual home," cut off from the source of shelter, rest, and belonginess?[13] How have we experienced God when we packed our bags and journeyed to a distant place? Have we somehow sensed God's sorrow and pained heart as we chose to look elsewhere for love, acceptance, and affirmation only to find them all wanting? Whatever the answer we might have for these questions, remember, our queer God still loves us regardless.

The queer father waited patiently for the return of the prodigal son, and when he finally did, the unexpected happened. The imminent reunion is described quite poignantly: "But while he was still far off, his father saw him and was filled with compassion; he ran and put his arms around him and kissed him." The father perhaps had waited and watched every day for his son to come home, for he knew in his heart what would befall him. He knew what the village folk might do to his son for bringing shame and dishonor to the family, and he was "determined to reach the boy before he reaches the village . . . and he must see him at a great distance" so he could protect him from getting treated badly.[14]

One day, the long wait finally ended. The father saw his son at a great distance in rags, emaciated, perhaps even unrecognizable at first glance—except to him. When his longing eyes rested on his son's gaunt figure, he was filled with compassion and ran to him and embraced and kissed him. The distance created by the selfish choices the son had made were bridged by the warmth of his father's unconditional, expressive, compassionate love.

In Middle Eastern culture, men with status and means did not run in public.[15] It was unbecoming for them because their legs would have been exposed. Still, buoyed by his excitement and deep yearning to touch, soothe, and caress his long lost and wearied son, he ran, defying cultural injunction. His display of vulnerability, of letting himself be subjected to public humiliation for his subversive ways, did not stop there. He took it to a whole new level by embracing and kissing his son without hesitation, making the "cost of his love *visible* in a public drama."[16]

Surprised by his father's visible expression of compassionate love, the son offered words of contrition, as he had rehearsed, with the hope that he could work his way to becoming his father's son again. But the father had something outrageous in mind. The son who wished him dead was restored back to his rightful place in his father's household. He was clothed with the best robe and given a ring and sandals. His father gave him his sonship back by giving him "honor (the best robe), trust (a signet ring), and self-respect (sandals)."[17]

With his son's return and restoration, there was one thing left to do: throw a huge feast by killing a fatted calf, for this son of his "was dead and is alive again; he was lost and is found." The celebration, with everyone in the village invited, was symbolic of the father's joy and intent to reconcile his son with all of them.

Another Interlude

Some of us may still be wandering in a far-off place, distanced from our spiritual home. Like the prodigal son, some may still be contemplating what to say to our queer God when we take the first step in our journey back home. We may be on our knees expressing our contrite heart. Wherever we are in this journey, our queer God waits and watches patiently for our return. There is no emotional blackmail or guilt-tripping or hurried gestures to have us back in the fold. God's costly love includes not impinging upon our freedom. That we know in our reading of this parable.

When we do return, what might we anticipate God to do? In what way does God run toward us? How has God extended the warmth of divine embrace and kiss? Simply, how have we experienced God's presence during times of limits and through the vicissitudes of our lives? As heirs of God's queerdom and because of God's overflowing generosity, how might we respond to God bestowing upon us "honor, trust, and self-respect?" Would we accept this offer wholeheartedly and in humility? Would we accept that we were once dead to sin but are now alive in Jesus Christ? That we were also once lost—or perhaps still are—but now have been found by God, who, like a shepherd, is searching for the lost sheep? Or might there still be residual desire to earn our way through this? Whatever our responses might be and wherever we are in this journey, remember that our queer God loves us, no matter what.

The queer Father, after receiving what looked like a scolding from the older son in front of their guests, subverted expectation yet again with gentle endearment, quiet love, and joyful reception of a new life. "My son" (another translation has "beloved son") were the first words uttered to counter his son's burning rage. Here, affection met indignation, and quiet, reassuring love cradled anger and resentment. He knew that the oldest heir was as lost as the younger, wandering in the prickly land of envy, competition, and perceived unlovability. He sensed his growing hostility but chose to access the deep hurt that fueled all this negativity. And when the anger was reprocessed into grace, he reassured the lost older son that his physical proximity to his father meant proximity to all—presence, privileges, and uninterrupted provisions.[18] Though he could not recognize all this, his father's steady commitment to loving him in all ways had not and would not change.

Rather than letting his son drown in self-righteousness or a sense of misplaced entitlement, the father lifted him up to see and hopefully join the hearty celebration in honor of the return of his younger brother. The emphasis here is on the relationship between the two brothers, with the older brother being nudged to extend an empathic and joyful reception to the younger one, who "was dead and is alive again; he was lost and is found." This was not an ordinary homecoming. The party was not just any other party in the village. Something of great significance had happened—shalom had been recovered back in the household.[19]

Last Interlude

When are those moments when we feel like railing at God? What is it like to break our heart open in the same way as the older son in the parable? How has God accompanied us during those times? What have we heard or sensed from God? What is it like to live as heirs of God's queerdom? What spiritual inheritance has God made available for us? How have we been stewarding this? What is obstructing our enjoyment of it? How might we celebrate and rejoice in the return of our siblings in the fold? Would we join the party and revel in the gift of shalom bestowed so graciously on us by God? However we think about these questions or feel toward God in certain moments of our lives, know that our God loves us, no matter what.

Perhaps as we lean into this story, we may discover that we too as queer folk who have been on the inside of God's ken—mediating Immanuel ("God with us") and icons of the Trinity ("a window into the spacious, gratuitous, and transforming love of God")—are being called, invited, nudged, lured, empowered to be like the queer father, mother, or parent in the parable. If so, what might this look like in the quotidian queer life? How might our relationships be different if we allow this queerness to imbue our ways of being with them? And when the love we offer is rejected or missed, we can still choose to love them, no matter what.

So, let's throw a party and the theme or category is Love Extravaganza.

CHAPTER 8

NEIGHBORLY LOVE

The Parable of the Good Samaritan

Luke 10:25–37

An expert in the law stood up to test Jesus. "Teacher," he said, "what must I do to inherit eternal life?" He said to him, "What is written in the law? What do you read there?" He answered, "You shall love the Lord your God with all your heart and with all your soul and with all your strength and with all your mind and your neighbor as yourself." And he said to him, "You have given the right answer; do this, and you will live."

But wanting to vindicate himself, he asked Jesus, "And who is my neighbor?" Jesus replied, "A man was going down from Jerusalem to Jericho and fell into the hands of robbers, who stripped him, beat him, and took off, leaving him half dead. Now by chance a priest was going down that road, and when he saw him, he passed by on the other side. So likewise a Levite, when he came to the place and saw him, passed by on the other side. But a Samaritan while traveling came upon him, and when he saw him he was moved with compassion. He went to him and bandaged his wounds, treating them with oil and wine. Then he put him on his own animal, brought him to an inn, and took care of him. The next day he took out two denarii, gave them to the innkeeper, and said, 'Take care of him, and when I come back I will repay you whatever more you spend.' Which of these three, do you think, was a neighbor to the man who fell into the hands of the robbers?" He said, "The one who showed him mercy." Jesus said to him, "Go and do likewise."

As the protagonist in the story, queer followers of Christ take on the call to care for those who are hurting—from individual relations to faith communities—not from a place of strength but out of the depths of pain we have endured from the hands of both robbers and religious authorities.

Breathe

We have heard the story before, perhaps countless times. A man was robbed and left for dead on the side of the street. Stripped of his dignity and belongings, he lay there wounded, alone, and half dead (Luke 10:30), perhaps groaning in pain and pleading for help. Wait a minute. These few lines are eerily familiar, because this parable plays out in real life among queer folk all too frequently.

- Brandon Teena: assaulted, gang-raped, then stabbed to death

- Matthew Shephard: robbed, tortured, and tied to a barbed-wire fence and left to die

- Tony MacDade: misgendered, attacked, falsely accused, and then fatally shot

- Dominique "Rem'mmie" Fells: her mangled body found on a riverbank with both legs severed

- Jennifer Laude: found with her head in a toilet bowl and died because of asphyxiation by drowning

The list continues, though many of these senseless deaths didn't make the news. By considering their deaths not newsworthy, their lives have been erased and their deaths were deemed not worth mourning. There is no end to the killings of queer folk, it seems, leaving the rest of our community, especially queer people of color, under the shadow of death, which is lurking, imposing, and ferocious to no end. So in defiance and in remembrance of the beautiful souls of our queer beloveds, we utter these phrases:

#saytheirnames

#queerlivesANDdeathsDOcount

#B R E A T H E

Yes, let us take a few gentle, deep breaths.

Bystanding

The appalling scene that begins the parable would cause anyone witnessing this dire situation to act hurriedly to save the wounded man. Right? Anyone? Well, not really—not even usually—according to this story.

The first witness to this event was a priest who saw the ailing man but chose to look the other way and "passed by on the other side." The wounded one's groans and cry for help fell on deaf ears. His bruised body was no match for the priest's allegiance to his religious duty; he was willing to sacrifice the life of another to guarantee that he remained ceremonially clean so he could offer sacrifices in the temple (cf. Mark 3:1–6).

Then another temple representative came along, a Levite. He saw the wounded man but also looked the other way and "passed by on the other side"—this from another religious man who, despite his proximity, chose to distance himself from the suffering of others and justified it somehow as an acceptable form of worship. Two passersby supposedly were mediators between God and humans and were conduits of God's mercy and compassion, but the situation remained unchanged, or perhaps worse, for the man in the ditch. He still lay there fighting for dear life.

Then a Samaritan—an outsider—arrived on the scene and did the unthinkable. He stopped to help. Unlike the priest and the Levite, the Samaritan "took pity on him" when he saw the wounded man. The depth of his care, attention, and empathy played out in his actions. The Samaritan bandaged his wounds, pouring on oil and wine. Then he put the man on his own donkey, brought him to a nearby inn, and took care of him.

Let us parse this intentional act of neighborly love, a kind of love that requires proximity to those suffering, offers practical help, and ensures a continuity of care that involves others. Here compassion is displayed in the concreteness of the Samaritan's engaged witness, response, and action.

But there's more.

Queering the parable uncovers other layers. First, it exposes the religious authorities' true allegiance, especially when forced to choose between holy customs (i.e., observing purity laws) and holy acts (i.e., observing the law of love). The latter, as the story goes, disappears and the former takes center stage.

Second, the parable also unmasks the never-ending supply of privilege and affordances that people with "divine power" (or anyone in or who has power, for that matter) have in determining what warrants their attention, appearance, or active engagement. Endowed with the power to choose that which benefits them and have that choice legitimized by virtue of their "divine appointment," their privilege is wielded at every turn. Those whose lives and deaths are deemed unworthy of grief are left only to choose between surviving, depending on others, or dying a slow and painful death.

Power, privilege, and holy posturing do not operate in a vacuum. In fact, the psychology of bystanding reveals or "allows the status quo distributions of power and privilege to go unchecked."[1] By seeing and then passing by on the other side—an intentional act of avoidance, of keeping what is visible invisible, of pretending to not fully grasp the call for help or understanding the meanings of what one sees—bystanding then becomes a clear collusion with the unjust, uncaring, and unaffected social and religious order and hierarchy.

Simply, this parable is about unveiling the structure that supports a cult or culture of moral and spiritual bankruptcy. Putting the priest and the Levite at the beginning of the first act is strategic. Easily identified as belonging to a community of temple personnel, their place in the parable can be seen as an unapologetic indictment of the power of groupthink in shaping and sculpting the behaviors of their ilk.

And then we have the good Samaritan, the queer good Samaritan.

The words *good* and *Samaritan* were not usually paired together given the explosive racialized tension between Jews and Samaritans during the time of Jesus. And yet in this parable, Jesus used a despised foreigner to be an exemplar of compassion or neighborly love. The ones who are usually dismissed, discarded, even desecrated are now sacralized, cherished, and catapulted to the place of honor. Here lies the difference: whereas these religious professionals are wedded to their legalism and optics, the despised perpetual foreigner embodies love that is gratuitous, unconditional, and knows no bounds—the "Jesus-figure" in the parable. In a nutshell the story of the good Samaritan is a story of neighborly love that is scandalous in its inclusivity, outrageous in its display of concern, and radical in its generosity. Very queer indeed.

But don't hide behind the shadow of the good Samaritan just yet or bask in our capacity to empathize because of our shared experience as the "other." Though many times we have been attacked, discarded, or robbed of our humanity, we too have walked the path of self-righteousness like the priest and the Levite. In other words, our queer lives contain traces of the dominant, the dominated, and the divine in the parable.

The dominant queer. This is probably a not-so-well-kept secret but certainly well-protected clique within the queer community. In queer hierarchy, we encounter the MEOWs—moneyed, educated, ostensibly cis-male, and white or some other blends—who sit at the apex of the pyramid. Their agenda usually takes primacy, their voices are heard loudly, and their elite activism is at times intolerant and unforgiving.

The bottom of the pyramid is wide and dense, stacked with Black and Brown bodies, yet their presence is often rendered invisible. Their queer lives teeter between anonymity and silence, precarity and death. And in this stratified existence, it is easier for those at the top to be blinded by their own myopic "gay agenda" and become oblivious to or dismissive of the plight of those at the bottom. Like the priest and Levite in the parable, this privileged position within the queer hierarchy grants the MEOWs many choices, while others are only given one choice—either to live (while staying in the closet or being surveilled or incarcerated) or die.

Lord, Have Mercy

The dominated queer. The assault on queer life never ceases. Like the nameless victim in the parable, we also have been physically bruised and beaten, robbed of human dignity, and discarded like waste that litters the altar of the sacred. And we carry this within our wearied bodies, scarred psyches, and famished souls *all the time*. Though some have found solace and a lifeline, many still wander on the streets, have gone back to the closet, or are drowning in pills and booze and sex to self-medicate. Worse, numerous lives are still cut short violently at the hands of the cis/heterosexual mob. The grievous yet, considered by society, ungrievable deaths of the Brandon Teena or the Dominique Fells or the Jennifer Laude in our midst are a testament to this grim reality that haunts us and should propel us into action.

For those of us who live under a religious canopy, the curtailment, erasure, and exclusion of and violence toward the queer life "in the name of God" is the ultimate form of spiritual abuse and trauma. In Rene Girard's analysis, violence that is intimately tied to the sacred or projected onto God is called *sacred violence*. But any justification of violence committed in the name of God does not come from the true God, for the "actual initiative to kill does not originate in God after all, but in human beings attacking one another."[2] As harsh as this truth is, we humans are perpetual attackers of each other. And this doesn't have to be always literal, of course. The refusal to see or bear witness to the suffering of others is a subtle yet pervasive and death-inducing form of sacred violence.

Ziggy, a queer clergyperson of color in the United Methodist Church, grew up in "a very conservative Methodist family," studied in "conversative Bible schools," and lived and played surrounded by pastors of the same religious persuasion. Coinciding with this early formation was his gradual sexual awakening and the confusion he experienced when trying to navigate the tension and conflict between his queer desires and those imposed by religious dogma.

> I had issues with this because even at ten years old I already knew there was a stigma about being gay. Even at this age, and since I was being groomed for ministry, I had access to 1972 *Book of Discipline* that contained very clear language about homosexuality being incompatible with Christianity. So, growing up I hid and protected myself by being in the closet to the point that I was harming other queer people and being a bully toward them.

The sacred violence he experienced "in the name of God" at a very young age left him maimed and disconnected not only from himself but from those who like him yearned for acceptance, belongingness, and affirmation of call to ministry. The scar was invisible to many, but the pain he experienced was incalculable. This left Ziggy utterly alone and lonely.

But time and time again, the transformative and revelatory power of the Christ event cannot be suppressed or tightly contained. It is bound to break through this coverup and reveal, once and for all, the deception of sacred violence. God has nothing to do with this violence.

And this was the experience of Ziggy. In a tearful confession, almost a declaration, he offered this:

My first church appointment as an ordained clergy was the very same church that I was baptized in. When I preached at that church for the first time, I was having a side conversation with God. And this was what I heard: "You had many questions and I seemed silent, but I walked with you full circle from this place where I took you in my church, celebrated you in your baptism, and affirmed you—*you are my child.* You have been surrounded by my grace ever since I walked with and journeyed with you. And now you are here, you are here as my servant, you are mine, and there is *nothing* wrong with you."

Come, Lord Jesus, come.

The Divine Queer

The divine queer takes its cue from the queer example of the good Samaritan. The motif of reversal in the parable, which renders the "despised Samaritan the hero and the Bible-believing-and-obeying priest and Levite the villains" is framed and deployed within the context of an interesting exchange between an expert in Jewish law and Jesus.[3] "What must I do to inherit eternal life?" asked the lawyer (v. 25). The intent of his questioning is dubious and seems deliberately designed to test Jesus. Sensing the lawyer's hidden motive, Jesus replied with questions of his own: "What is written in the law? What do you read there?" (v. 26). Not to be outwitted, of course, the lawyer retorted by citing the great commandment from Deuteronomy 6:5, "You shall love the Lord your God with all your heart and with all your soul and with all your might," and, Leviticus 19:18, "You shall love your neighbor as yourself" (v. 27). This is the heart of Jewish law, and both Jesus and the lawyer knew that.

Satisfied with the lawyer's answer, Jesus admonished him to translate the heart of this law into a life lived in love, and he would inherit eternal life (v. 28), of living in communion with God not in the distant past but in the concreteness of his life—of our lives—right here right now. But the lawyer was unrelenting. Unnerved by the simple yet profound answer of Jesus, he asked, "And who is my neighbor?" (v. 29). As someone well versed in Torah and therefore acquainted with its many laws requiring Israelites to show mercy to everyone without limits and conditions, this question was brimming with prejudice and a hidden agenda. The question "Who is my neighbor?" was his way of "asking Jesus to interpret the Torah as to the kinds of people Jesus would exclude from his love."[4]

Much to the lawyer's dismay, Jesus answered not with a straightforward statement, but with a story of the good Samaritan that turned his religious world upside down. As the unlikely hero of the story, the despised Samaritan, who knew the law of love fulfilled it wholeheartedly through his concrete acts of mercy and compassion, became the epitome of what it truly means to love one's neighbor as oneself.

As Jesus-loving queer folk, our status within our faith community (at least generally speaking) is like that of the Samaritan—despised, othered, an outcast. And yet we have been and are called to continue to live into the inclusive love of God through our acts of hospitality, generosity, and engaged compassion. We can participate in this incarnational ministry of loving mimesis or imitation right where we are, wherever we may be.

Stretching us beyond our pain and suffering, Jesus calls us not only to live out our queerness without apology, but to love queerly, to be queer good Samaritans. The scars we carry in our psyches, bodies, and souls can be and have been a balm to soothe the pain of others. This shared pain can be a wellspring of empathic connection and engaged compassion to prod us along on this lifelong journey of healing and restoration. This is what infuses Ziggy's abiding and steadfast commitment to supporting the flourishing of the queer community within a denomination that pays homage to sacred violence instead of following the way of love.

Loving queerly also means working with our allies to rebuild our faith communities that have been co-opted by the larger and social realm of principalities and powers that operate around and is sustained by the mechanism of exclusion. We can pattern our response after the example of Jesus, who took the temple system to account because it had unchained itself from its sacred call and who challenged its entanglements with the economic and political power of the time. We can also call into question and subvert the practice of institutionalism where the priority is placed on survival, order, security, and peace and to recapture what it means for the church to become God's instantiation here on earth, through our radical hospitality and scandalous inclusivity.[5]

Our faith communities also need our outrageous display of concern because they are also bleeding out and losing vitality to be witnesses to God's action in the world that is marked by never-ending division and conflicts, and war. Like the wounded man in the parable, our churches need our engaged compassion so that, along with others, we can provide an empathic and caring presence and sharing of resources to help in the restoration of the body of Christ. This restoration comes in the form of mediating the presence of God amid all the brokenness we see in our faith communities, even if we get rejected once more. When we are no longer run by a pattern of desire that seeks to engage us in the perpetual game of sacred violence, we can stand firm and remain steadfast in God's call to love our enemies (Matt. 5:44–45). Put another way, for loving mimesis to be a true reflection of Christ's cruciform love, we must also consider the liberation of those who have persecuted us and benefited from the exclusionary mechanism by loving them without conditions, because God does. They are our neighbors too.

• • •

After telling the story, Jesus reengaged the lawyer with a very simple yet direct question—"Which of these three, do you think, was a neighbor to the man who fell into the hands of robbers?" (v. 36)—to which he replied, "The one who showed him mercy" (v. 37). Challenging the lawyer beyond the confines of merely knowing the Torah, he admonished him to "go and do likewise" (v. 38), that is, to live his life like the good Samaritan.

In the same way, our queer God admonishes us to go and do likewise.

That is, let us live into our calling as queer Samaritans imbuing the theme or category (LOL) Loving Out Loud.

CHAPTER 9

QUEERS' GOT TALENT

The Parable of the Talents

Matthew 25:14–30

For it is as if a man, going on a journey, summoned his slaves and entrusted his property to them; to one he gave five talents, to another two, to another one, to each according to his ability. Then he went away. At once the one who had received the five talents went off and traded with them and made five more talents. In the same way, the one who had the two talents made two more talents. But the one who had received the one talent went off and dug a hole in the ground and hid his master's money. After a long time the master of those slaves came and settled accounts with them. Then the one who had received the five talents came forward, bringing five more talents, saying, "Master, you handed over to me five talents; see, I have made five more talents." His master said to him, "Well done, good and trustworthy slave; you have been trustworthy in a few things; I will put you in charge of many things; enter into the joy of your master." And the one with the two talents also came forward, saying, "Master, you handed over to me two talents; see, I have made two more talents." His master said to him, "Well done, good and trustworthy slave; you have been trustworthy in a few things; I will put you in charge of many things; enter into the joy of your master." Then the one who had received the one talent also came forward, saying, "Master, I knew that you were a harsh man, reaping where you did not sow, and gathering where you did not scatter seed, so I was afraid, and I went and hid your talent in the ground. Here you have what is yours." But his master replied, "You wicked and lazy slave! You knew, did you, that I reap where I did not sow and gather where I did not scatter? Then you ought to have invested my money with the bankers, and on my return I would have received what was my own with interest. So take the talent from him, and give it to the one with the ten

talents. For to all those who have, more
will be given, and they will have an abundance, but from those who have nothing, even what they have will be taken
away. As for this worthless slave, throw
him into the outer darkness, where there
will be weeping and gnashing of teeth."

*In this chapter the charisms of queer folk, which has long
been silenced and denied, are affirmed, celebrated, and
used as integral to the life and mission of the church. By
regarding them as trustworthy servants entrusted with
talents or gold, they become active participants in the
flourishing of others who make up the body of Christ.*

I love watching *America's Got Talent* (*AGT*), for it
showcases human skill and creativity in all its glorious
forms—from singing to dancing, from comedic rou-
tines to dog shows, from card tricks to spoken word,
and more. There is even a version of this popular show
in the Philippines that brings so much nostalgia and
pride for those of us in the diaspora. The two-minute
audition that gets shown on television does not give
justice to the countless hours of preparation, hard
work, social support, and self-belief that go into the
fleeting but awesome displays of great talent. The
competition is stiff, and the grand champion walks
away with $1 million and a gig in Las Vegas. Though
only one is crowned a winner, viewers get to root for
loads of talent.

Interestingly, the word *talent*, which we now use to refer to human ability, is derived from the parable of the talents that we are about to queer. Besides sharing that word and the common theme of rewarding hard work, the parable also intimates or signals something of queer life and faith—and, as an aside, queer folk have graced the stage of *AGT*.

Freedom or Fear

The parable of the talents has elicited a variety of interpretations. Some see the man as one who went on a journey as a stand-in for Christ ascending to heaven and dispensing rewards and punishments on his return. The story has also been used as a scriptural support for stewardship, in that hard work and faithfulness are rewarded and lack of it leads to loss. The most common approach to the parable is directed toward the disciples "to encourage kingdom living" while they wait for Christ's return.[1]

The narrative structure of the parable, like the others explored in this book, invites a more curious reading. The first line—"if a man, going on a journey, summoned his slaves and entrusted his property to them"—invokes a test that deals with overseeing or managing financial matters. The wealth is divided into five, two, and one talents between the master's three servants. In the ancient world, a talent weighed around sixty to ninety pounds and was the equivalent of six thousand days of wages for a day laborer.[2] Hence, the man with five talents was given a huge amount of money, and even the one with a single talent still had a sizable sum to steward. The servants who acted as the master's representatives were not slaves, because slaves would not have had the powers to make commercial transactions.[3]

The first two servants did not waste time doubling what was entrusted to them. The man who received five talents put his money to work and gained five more. Likewise, the one with two talents gained two more. Their efforts reflected their personal stake in their actions: they expected their master to reward them by sharing some of the profit each had made.[4]

The third servant had a different idea. He went off, dug a hole, and hid his master's money. Compared to the other two servants, at least on the surface, his decision to bury the talent put him in an awkward and unenviable position. He appeared to lack business acumen. But not so. Some sources consider his ways "prudent and trustworthy,"[5] even appropriate because he was protecting his master's money from getting lost or stolen. However, the wealth given to him was not for safekeeping; he was supposed to use it to create profit.[6] The servant's risk-averse decision merited an interesting exchange with his master, as we shall see later.

This story fits in the category of departure–return parables,[7] which is to say it starts off with a man departing on a journey and then returning to settle accounts. Perhaps proud of what they had accomplished, the first two servants came forward with a report of their successes, which were met with the master's approval, affirmation, and a promotion.

> Then the one who had received the five talents came forward, bringing five more talents, saying, "Master, you handed over to me five talents; see, I have made five more talents." His master said to him, "Well done, good and trustworthy slave; you have been trustworthy in a few things; I will put you in charge of many things; enter into the joy of your master." And the one with the two talents also came forward, saying, "Master, you handed over to me two talents; see, I have made two more talents." His master said to him, "Well done, good and trustworthy slave; you have been trustworthy in a few things; I will put you in charge of many things; enter into the joy of your master." (vv. 20–23)

The exchange represents a "moment of judgment." The meeting was a reckoning of the choices they had made with the task given to them. They were commended because of their faithfulness to their master. The oft-quoted line (in contemporary church life)— "Well done, good and faithful servant"—underscores the virtue they have shown as a steward.[8] Their promotion was a testament to their master's belief in their capabilities and the happiness he felt seeing them succeed and flourish.

The third servant had a different, and difficult, conversation with the master. He shifted the focus away from himself and "read" or called out the master by saying, "Master, I knew that you were a harsh man, reaping where you did not sow and gathering where you did not scatter, so I was afraid, and I went and hid your talent in the ground. Here you have what is yours" (vv. 24–25). There was a tinge of judgment in the servant's words, and then, appealing perhaps to the master's sensibility, he explained that his inaction was a result of fear. But then he postured himself to be cautious and blameless and acted as though he expected a commendation for being careful and honest.[9]

The master's response to the last servant was swift. Instead of dispensing commendation as he had done to the first two servants, he "read" the servant back, suggested what he could have done instead, took away the only talent he had been given, and banished him.

The judgment on the third servant seems harsh; perhaps the punishment doesn't fit the crime. But if we look at the intent of many of Jesus's departure-return parables, the master's departure is a test of faithfulness and follow-through on the task given. More pointedly, the parable acts as a description of the kind of demand the queerdom makes on its people: to not live in fear, that is, neither to act as a "preserver nor as one afraid; but act boldly he [*sic*] must . . . [force] a hearer to choose a future in which to live—for freedom."[10] Our queering of the parable will focus on that theme.

Queer Creativity

In ways both known and unknown to people in the church, queer folk have always "done church." We have been Sunday school and Bible teachers, organists and choir directors, youth and lay leaders, pastoral counselors and caregivers, pastors and church administrators, district superintendents, bishops, and faithful members. We have sat in the pews and sung all the hymns, received and celebrated the Eucharist, shared family potlucks, grieved together, joined in weddings and baptisms, celebrated birthdays and retirement parties, and prayed with and struggled through life's many twists and turns together. Yet too often, the moments when we have fully lived into our humanity as queer folk, we have become persona non grata; we have been banished because of our sexuality and gender identity. At times, we have also been welcomed (or tolerated) in some of these spaces, but we have not been fully affirmed and celebrated as queer faithful followers of God. Even when our creativity has been used (or abused), our personhood has been buried.[11]

Still, we have continued to find a way to be creative and grow the talents we have been entrusted to steward. We are queer, and we are here to stay come hell or high water. Some of us have walked away from church to heal or to find alternative and affirming spaces, but no bylaws or procedures, theology, or institutional structures can deter us from exercising our God-ordained call to ministry in all its manifold and creative expressions.

Having said that, it is important to recognize that creativity is not a queer gift reserved only for us. We are not more creative or imaginative than the next person. We are not genetically predisposed to envision and execute unconventional ideas. Even though the queer community is overrepresented in artistic and creative endeavors, studies find no evidence of a correlation between queer identity and creativity.[12] How, then, do we account for the proliferation of creative people among our community?

We are like a phoenix rising from the ashes. Belonging to a social and sexual minority group, we are constantly pushed to find alternative ways to fully express ourselves, to chase after our needs and our desires, to go underground to create a ballroom culture or queer sacred spaces, to cleanse ourselves from toxic and compulsory masculinity through drag in all its fabulous forms, and to recast the masculine white male deity into someone who transcends gender and whose image we bear—our queer God.

In other words, our marginalization drives our creativity as we test the boundaries set by the dominant culture to create something new, different, odd, strange, unfamiliar, disturbing, discomforting, and disorienting to create an inclusive and just world. The qualities that spark queer creativity include bold-ness, courage, freedom, spontaneity, integration, and self-acceptance.[13] We have no shortage of these qual-ities, not because we are born with them, but because we have had to learn how to harness them early on so we could survive and thrive in a man's white world. Our view of the world is oblique. We experience it differently, "and the art we create to voice ourselves speaks that difference. Society may not have the words necessary to speak our experience at times, so we find other ways like art and perhaps this familiarity with the different avenues of expression sets us apart."[14]

We also create to return to our bodies, which hold our dreams as well as fears, our integrity and our doubts, our possibilities and our limits. Perhaps, for many of us, this act of creation is a sort of homecoming, a return to a space familiar to us, a space that allows us to imagine wildly and unapologetically, a space where we can breathe freely and rediscover ourselves anew. In this way, the act of creation breathes new ways of being in a world that refuses to let us be. For spiritually oriented queers, creating is a way of connecting with the Creator who constantly tries to upend the ways of the world still stuck in a system that privileges the few and subjugates the different. The creations of queer folk provide a glimpse of a world beyond the one we inhabit and make present the future that is still to come. Gifted with the Spirit of Christ, our passion to participate in the unfolding of this new creation comes out of our experience of injustice, cruelty, violence, and shame. Though we have been reduced to ashes, the Spirit within sparks new energy, visions, and creations that allow us to take flight like a phoenix.

Like the first two servants in the parable, we have multiplied the talents we were given to steward. Unlike them, the road to doubling has not always been easy or straightforward, yet we managed somehow to be creative amid unremitting messages of hate and disapproval of both our work and our worth. In this space of liminality, we find our groove, the vibe that propels us to keep going regardless of the outcome.

Perhaps in the parable the profit came only as a result of the servants' faithfulness to the master's instructions and their own sense of agency. It is the same for queer folk. It is always an uphill climb, yet we press on, inspired by our self-belief and the encouragement of our queer siblings.

Like the third servant, at times we are paralyzed by fear and trauma that make it difficult for us to do much more than dig a hole and bury the talent or shy away from spaces that will make us even more vulnerable and precarious. That is not a statement of judgment. The third servant serves as a warning not to succumb to the forces, both internal and external, that try to snuff out the flickering flame that remains in us. In the waiting period is an opportunity to heal, to rest, to be reborn so we can crawl out from under the rubble of fear and passivity to reclaim our spot with the rest of God's creation.

Words That Heal

"Well done, good and faithful servant."

Those are words we long to hear. They are the same words we have often been deprived of hearing because our work and worth have been judged according to the standards of a cis/heterosexist white gaze. Yet the parable comes to us as good news. It assures us that these words have already been spoken to us by God, perhaps as a gentle whisper that sometimes get crowded out by the noise within and the nonsensical chatter by those who consider themselves superior spiritual emissaries.

In God's gaze faithfulness comes first. The parable, which is set within the context of Jesus's teaching about the queerdom and the future, draws the hearer and reader to the importance of faithfulness and issues a warning against unfaithfulness. The parable "anticipates passage of time when faithfulness is necessary,"[15] and where our true character, motivation, and commitment to following the liberative ways of God will be put to a test. Perhaps we are living in those days right now.

We have the perfect example in Christ, who remained faithful until the very end, unperturbed by religious and political conspiratorial acts that sought to undermine his message and ministry. Though his own received him not (John 1:11) and his disciples deserted him during his hour of need, he remained faithful and obedient even unto death. Because of this,

God exalted him to the highest places and gave him the name above all names so that every knee would bow to worship him (Phil. 2:9–11)—a fitting coronation that parallels the message in the parable, where the reward comes after a steadfast display of faithfulness.

For most queer folk, this may not come as a surprise given the centrality of the kind of atonement theory we were exposed to in our spiritual formation. At the same time, it might be worth remembering that Christ's *via dolorosa* or way of suffering mirrors, though is not equivalent to, the kind of path queer folk have to tread—a path of discomfort, pain, alienation, and exclusion. Like Christ, we have endured thorns and thistles, encountered blocks and detours, yet we have remained faithful to God's call. Our faithfulness isn't confined to a particular expression, especially a religious one; our call is not limited to a particular form of ministry, though many of us have chosen that path. Our faithfulness is to God and to whatever God has called us to be and do.

Every time you create out of joy, lean into the words, "You are good and faithful! Well done!"

Every time you create out of the depths of your pain, hear this: "You are good and faithful! Well done!

Relish every win, triumph, victory, and reward, whatever the size or the occasion. Incline your ears to these words: "You are good and faithful! Well done!

When you fall or are pushed to fall and you need time to recover and heal, remember: "You are good and faithful! Well done!"

When your queerness brings forth fruit, celebrate in the knowledge that "you are good and faithful! Well done!"

Remember, faithfulness is what matters in the end.

Let's create and multiply those talents and while we are at it let us embody the theme or category: Queer Faith as Avant-Garde Faith.

CHAPTER 10

QUEER CHRIST

The Parable of the Wise and Foolish Builders

Luke 6:47–49

I will show you what someone is like who comes to me, hears my words, and acts on them. That one is like a man building a house who dug deeply and laid the foundation on rock; when a flood arose, the river burst against that house but could not shake it because it had been well built. But the one who hears and does not act is like a man who built a house on the ground without a foundation. When the river burst against it, it quickly collapsed, and great was the ruin of that house.

This last meditation circles back to where the book started—an admonition to remain grafted to the True Vine, to listen attentively to the Good Shepherd, to stand on the chief cornerstone, the queer Christ. By standing on this sure foundation, queer folk are anchored firmly and fiercely amid the daily and unremitting challenges and obstacles that will continue to come our way.

It is fitting to end this book on queering the parables of Jesus with the parable of the wise and foolish builders. In a way, the preceding reflections are like spiritual columns supporting queer faith. Better yet, I hope that it has offered a spiritual sanctuary for you. And as in any structure, the columns, along with the rest of the components of the building structure, depend on a sturdy foundation to keep them steady and provide protection from the elements. In like manner, queer faith flourishes not merely through the active reception of the teachings (i.e., the hearing and doing of the words heard or read) of Christ, but also in putting our faith in the person of the queer Christ.

As we consider the parable, I want to focus on the images used by Jesus that mirror Isaiah 28:14–18, which has at its center God's promise of "laying in Zion a foundation stone, a tested stone, a precious cornerstone, a sure foundation." The prophet Isaiah

> had no confidence in the building
> they had built (the agreement with
> Egypt) and predicted that a great

storm was on its way (Assyria). That storm would destroy their building but in the future God would lay a new cornerstone in Zion that would be a sure foundation for a new building. The foundation would not be an ordinary rock but a gemstone. . . . To hear and to do my words, said Jesus, was to build on "the foundation" that Isaiah promised. In short, Jesus was saying, "I am the foundation stone. . . . Build on me and my words and you will not be shaken. Isaiah's parable of the destroyed building and the promised new foundation is not fulfilled in the Qumran or the second temple, but in me and my words."[1]

For most queer Christians, putting our faith in Christ has not always been a "sure foundation." In fact, the preferred interpretation of the foundation has been used to bruise and bury us because of who we are (and becoming) and whom we love. As they use this rock to clobber us, it becomes a badge of some sort, a testament to their allegiance to this "sacred work." As a result, queer seekers can develop "christophobia," or "a revulsion both toward all things Christian and toward Jesus Christ himself."[2] This evolves over time as a response to the relentless blast of oppressive discourse against queer sexuality and gender identity that renders our humanity—thoughts, feelings, desires, longings, intentions, and dreams, not just about our sexuality, but everything that constitutes our personhood—suspect, defective, unacceptable, and incompatible with Christian faith. These teachings have delegitimized the authenticity of our deepest longings to love, know, and serve God, which in turn has created a wide chasm between our bodily integrity and our deepest spiritual yearnings. Suffused with familiar biblical justifications and couched in shame and guilt, this oppressive discourse has scarred our souls and demonized our spirituality.[3]

How do we crawl back from under the rubble left by the ruins of exclusion and sacred violence to find faith to anchor ourselves on the chief cornerstone? Put another way, how do we separate Jesus who was "Hellenized, ontologized, spiritualized, depoliticized, and ecclesialized" from the Jesus who got down and dirty with those who were despised by and on the fringes of society?[4] How do we disentangle the sanitized Christ from the queer Christ who offers a different footing for us to stand on?

Queer Christ

But what does it mean to imagine Jesus Christ as queer in the first place? We need not look further than the Jesus portrayed in the Gospels who "lived and loved out loud" in radical ways. Never to be aligned with the elite, the haves, the power hungry, and the dominant, unless to rebuke them of their smugness and spiritual bankruptcy, the Jesus we encounter in the Gospel narratives is one who was unapologetically out and about with ordinary folk, dined with the so-called sinners and tax collectors, and stood beside a woman caught in adultery. He is one "who entered into immediate, shockingly unconventional relationship with people, not evading the human encounter by the choreography of socio-cultural role definitions."[5] A queer act indeed.

He not only lived out loud, but he loved so loudly that it stirred up the pious and the protectors of tradition so much that they tried to shove his fierce love back into the closet, much like the religious elite of our day who are eager to dispense judgment for any fraction of deviance from their established "holy orders." Their lust for blood, if you will, is linked to a theological perspective we have come to know as atonement theory, which focuses on the "sinful nature" of humanity that can only be redeemed by Jesus's sacrificial death. If we peel back this story, we discover a "deal whereby someone who was remote and angry remained remote and angry but created an exception for those lucky enough to be covered with the blood of his son"—a distant, angry God demanding sacrifice.[6] Those "covered with the blood" of Jesus have to "straighten their lives" to keep up their end of the deal—a strange mix of gratitude and fear.

Those outside of the Christianized cis/heterosexual norm must subject themselves to its prescribed beliefs and practices if they want to be saved. After all, "Jesus died for our sins," and his death is an expression of God's "unconditional love for us," so how dare we belittle this sacrificial act of Jesus by living as we wish? (By that I mean, living authentically.) The logic is ludicrous. This supposedly unconditional love is conditional through and through, and it capitalizes on guilt and shame, which chain queer Christians to psychological insanity and spiritual abuse. It is emotional blackmail—a twisted understanding of what Jesus's death and resurrection mean for us.

Part of unshackling the queer Christ from the sanitized Christ is to swing the closet wide open and center the "cross-ings" that Jesus did repeatedly to meet people like us where we are and as we are. Jesus is the motivation and inspiration that releases the queer community from the clutches of cis/heterosexism; Jesus is undeniably queer.[7] In fact, Jesus's focus on destabilizing and disrupting power structures and the relations that keep them entrenched is at the heart of what it means to be queer—the very foundation that will keep us grounded and anchored. This is the Jesus we need to be out. Better yet, we must allow this out Jesus to queer and query other versions of Jesus that have come down to us to see if they align with or distort the divine liberation that God has for us.

Integral to queering the Jesus we have inherited is to extract (or exorcise) the sanitized Jesus so deeply entrenched in our psyche that unconsciously thinks in a very straight manner and assumes that all society and religion is and must be straight. This means interrogating images, theologies, spiritualities, and all aspects of our meaning-making to see whether they support our flourishing or keep us subjugated in the service of the often "unquestioned principle of male as the norm, dominance/submission, hierarchy, and possession."[8]

This critical and soulful work can be facilitated in myriad ways. Let me describe briefly what this means. Queer work is always reflexive and critical, but to add soulfulness to this urgent work brings in another dimension—more "bodily and lived in": not simply cognitive but also sensory, not in isolation but in community, almost orgy-like in the sense that it allows for open and unrestricted dialogue about queer matters.

Lament often accompanies this soulful work given the pain and trauma we harbor in our bodies, which we must release as our way of consenting to live freely, authentically, and queerly. But there is also tenderness, perhaps extended to us by those who provide a shelter and a footing, which we can now offer ourselves as a gesture of self-love. And then gradually, perhaps, we can embrace fully the gift of our erotic desires and the carnality and sanctity of our bodies as our way of owning and celebrating our humanity in its manifold forms and expressions. This, in a way, is a form of resistance, the lived and living unapologetically in and through our queer body, which is

> more an attitude than a particular set of genitals and orientations. The queer Christian body is a transgressive

signifier of radical equality. It attempts
to subvert the weight of patriarchy
upon countercultural actions. This
body lives in the world but is not
chained by its narrow definitions and
hierarchical power systems. It is a
body that acts stubbornly in the face of
life as it is, and is a space in which creative rebellion is rooted in the everyday business of life. In the language of
Christianity, it is a redemptive space.[9]

Sanctified Queer Body

We need not hide or be ashamed of our bodies, or
mold them to fit the cis/heterosexual standard. Our
bodies are marked, signified, even singled out to make
manifest or signal what is possible, calling us back to
the *telos* or purpose of our existence as humans: to be
people invested in the flourishing of all and in all possible ways—bodily, psychologically, spiritually, relation-
ally both with people and the planet we share. Isn't this
why Jesus came in the first place? Not as a thief who
comes only to steal, kill, and destroy, which we humans
continue to do to one another, but as one who came
that we may have abundant life (John 10:10)—generous
in love, extravagant in how we treat one another and
how we care for the world. In our queer bodies standing securely on this foundation that is queer Christ, let

us lean in, again, as God says to us, "You are my beloved child, in whom I am well pleased" (Matt. 3:17, NKJV).

Our queer bodies that inhabits the world with fierceness and courage day in and day out are sanctified bodies, bearers of the image of God, icons of the spacious, transforming love of God that inflicts the comfortable and comforts the afflicted. It is not only a transgressive signifier of radical equality, but the queer body is also a transgressive signifier about what it means to be open, hospitable, affirming, and celebratory of the differences that make up the human community. In the process, our understanding of what it means to be human bearing the image of the queer God is queered, reshaped, and offered as a transgressive challenge to straight talk.[10] To put it more bluntly, our queer bodies open the cracks and make visible the crooked straight mind.

The political significance of this sanctified queer body is immense on another level. The normative cis/heterosexual body that has been rendered natural and sacred and is seen as the carrier of dominant values get all flustered, undone, and exposed when colliding with the sanctified queer body. The presence of queer bodies signal the uncomfortable, bitter truth that what has been marked as natural and sacred—that is, normative body—is actually a contorted, distorted, morphed version that serves social and religious hierarchy and worldly powers.[11] To put a stop to this crazymaking ruse, we rise in drag in all of its queer expressions if only to proclaim the futility and the devious agenda of playing, requiring, and acting straight.

In drag, we stand on the foundation that is the queer Christ. Theologically speaking, that means we have to rethink the significance of Jesus's crucifixion. The sacrificial atonement story that has been drilled into us as a way of "straightening out" our so-called disordered life and love isn't true. Instead, we need to see Jesus crossing over to our side and that there is something that is being done for, toward, or at us; we are undergoing something of great personal and cosmic significance, but it is not about sacrifice. It is an invitation to a new, strange, and unfamiliar way of being with ourselves and each other that does not involve self-degradation or revenge.[12]

This unfamiliar way of being-with is not something we can pull off on our own. Nor should we try to do so. We have been gifted with the Holy Spirit (Acts 2:38), who dwells within (Rom. 8:11), makes all things new (2 Cor. 5:17), and produces wisdom and revelation (Eph. 1:17) to help us discern with clarity the ways of Jesus from the ways of the world. The queer Christ has inducted us into a new way of life, a new vision for humanity, an "alternative vision of what human beings could be or are meant to be," in and through our queer body.[13]

The Mind of the Queer Christ

As we secure our spiritual sanctuary or home on a sure foundation, the chief cornerstone that is the queer Christ, we take on the mind of Christ, the antidote to the straight mind and everything it represents. The example of Jesus Christ as described vividly in Philippians 2 provokes us to focus on living rightly, that is, living in the pattern of Christ's love, which is one of radical hospitality and openness as God's Beloved and in our shared life with others as a beloved community, even with those who have wronged us. Again, we look to Christ's incarnation as the paradigm of what it means to empty ourselves of both imposed and fabricated shame and the desire to "otherize" those who have made us feel othered—unworthy and less than human—because of our queerness. The apostle Paul says it directly:

> In your relationships with one another,
> have the same mindset as Christ Jesus:
> Who, being in very nature God, did
> not consider equality with God some-
> thing to be used to his own advan-
> tage; rather, he made himself nothing
> by taking the very nature of a servant,
> being made in human likeness. And
> being found in appearance as a man,
> he humbled himself by becoming obe-
> dient to death on a cross!" (Phil. 2:5–8,
> NIV)

This call might feel strange and evocative of the pain associated with being forced to occupy a place of shame because of our sexuality and gender identity. In fact, it may even seem adversarial and contradictory to the myriad strategies of active resistance we have worked so hard to deploy. Those reservations are legitimate, even warranted. But there's another path we have not yet considered. Patterning ourselves after the mind of Christ and his self-emptying example does not mean giving up our agency. As imitators of Christ, we are instead admonished to give up our "lack of will to appropriate subjectivity, desire and agency as those made in the image of God" so we can love boldly and fiercely in the face of exclusion.[14]

Christ refused to grasp tightly to his nature or status or honor, and instead, he gave up everything so we can know the fullness of life. He was possessed with so much love that he gave up his place so we could be filled with the abundant gifts and fruits of the Spirit that are meant to be shared gratuitously, unconditionally, with others. He took the form of a slave so we can be freed from the cycle of enslaving ourselves and others or "inter-human violence."[15] He made all this possible not to shame us or make us feel indebted to him but to invite us into treating each other as image bearers of a loving, forgiving, and compassionate God.

As the mind of Christ takes hold in us, we also gradually discover that his descent on the "downward path of dishonor, suffering, and self-renouncing love" is also his way of entering the depths of human vulnerability and, by extension, directly experiencing the very depth of our own brokenness, suffering, and alienation.[16] Though we may feel alone, we are not. Truly. Though we may feel abandoned, we are accompanied. Always. Though we may feel unworthy, we are loved. Guaranteed. Though these promises may seem so far off at times and our feelings and wounds so overwhelming we cannot see past them, God's regard for us does not and will never change.

The Sure Foundation

The foundation, in other words, is secure and can withstand the torrent of storms and winds that will come our way. We know that the flood of assault on queer bodies and communities has happened, it is happening now, and it will continue to happen in the foreseeable future. We have exposed the crack both in the straight mind and the structure that support it. Defensively, the straight culture will try to contain this by creating a false sense of unanimity and belongingness among their adherents against us, and they will stop at nothing to ensure their privileged and normative status.

The parable's central message is clear and urgent: everyone who hears the words of the queer Christ and puts them in practice is like a wise builder who builds a house on the rock (Matt. 7:24). In the Palestinian context, villagers built stone houses only in the summer. Under a scorching sun, they did the backbreaking work of digging until they hit solid rock.[17]

In like manner, embodying the words of Christ take similar energy, intentionality, and focused attention to find that secure foundation. Digging through deeply entrenched beliefs and practices may be new to some queer folk or a daily practice for others. But the work is necessary, and we do not shy away from it. In fact, it is something we must do constantly just to protect our sanity and the flickering flame that keeps our hearts ablaze for God.

We will falter at times, wobble, and perhaps fall. Yet, the foundation and the chief cornerstone remains steady and firm. The queer Christ is steady and firm in his regard for us, steady and firm in his love that knows no conditions, and steady and firm to lift us up so we can continue this journey of claiming liberation and flourishing for all. I am also reminded of Paul's bold claim that "neither death nor life, neither angels nor demons, neither the present nor the future, nor any powers, neither height nor depth, nor anything else in all creation, will be able to separate us from the love of God that is in Christ Jesus our Lord" (Rom. 8:38–39, NIV). The gratuitous love that is made available to us, that is already present in us, that is already at work in us precedes our failings, rejoices in our victories, and eagerly waits for when everything and everyone becomes wholeheartedly and madly queer. That is where the security of the foundation lies; it rests solely in the love of God in Christ.

Let's start building on our foundation inspired by the theme or category: Queer All the Way.

QUEER DIVINE

The Man among the Tombs[1]

Luke 8:26–37

Then they arrived at the region of the
Gerasenes, which is opposite Galilee. As
he stepped out on shore, a man from
the city who had demons met him. For a
long time he had not worn any clothes,
and he did not live in a house but in the
tombs. When he saw Jesus, he cried
out and fell down before him, shouting,
"What have you to do with me, Jesus, Son
of the Most High God? I beg you, do not
torment me," for Jesus had commanded
the unclean spirit to come out of the man.
(For many times it had seized him; he
was kept under guard and bound with
chains and shackles, but he would break

the bonds and be driven by the demon into the wilds.) Jesus then asked him, "What is your name?" He said, "Legion," for many demons had entered him. They begged him not to order them to go back into the abyss.

Now there on the hillside a large herd of swine was feeding, and the demons begged Jesus to let them enter these. So he gave them permission. Then the demons came out of the man and entered the swine, and the herd stampeded down the steep bank into the lake and was drowned.

When the swineherds saw what had happened, they ran off and told it in the city and in the country. Then people came out to see what had happened, and when they came to Jesus, they found the man from whom the demons had gone sitting at the feet of Jesus, clothed and in his right mind. And they became frightened. Those who had seen it told them how the one who had been possessed by demons had been healed. Then the whole throng of people of the surrounding region of the Gerasenes asked Jesus to leave them, for they were seized with great fear. So he got into the boat and returned.

The miracles of Jesus can be seen as "parables in event," which is to say they speak in the same language as the stories. There is more going on than what is on the surface.

The experience of all-against-one is nothing new. Time and again, the queer community has been demonized anew and pushed to live among the dead, to be chained by the shackles of cis/hetero-patriarchy. It is embedded in our culture, our faith communities, and our close relations. In this gospel story we witness an encounter between Jesus the Exorcist and the one whom we have come to know as the Gerasene demoniac. For quite some time, this man had been the repository of an evil spirit, Legion, they are called, for they are many. Because of the Gerasene demoniac's unrestrained strength, the townsfolk were unable to subdue him; he constantly broke free of his chains and was driven to live in the graveyard among the tombs.

The man recognized Jesus, ran, fell at his feet, and begged Jesus not to torture him. He had only known himself as the town's outcast—the "other," or as James Alison describes him, "someone who represents what is not them, all that is dangerous, unsavory, and evil."[2] All that possessed the man pleaded not to be sent out of the country. Without him, Legion ceased to exist. They needed a receptacle, a container, a body to hold their individual and collective shame, guilt, and compulsions, something to hold their ostracized identity.

Jesus wasn't threatened by the man or his request. He asked their name because he knew Legion would self-destruct once their identity was unmasked—that is, once they no longer had a scapegoat.[3] The encounter was not only an encounter of liberation, but also one of transformation, a restoration of the other's full humanity. Everyone saw a man consumed by a demon become the "human vessel of God's divinity"—sitting at Jesus's feet, "clothed and in his right mind" (Luke 8:35).

But that's not the end of the story. The townsfolk were not relieved when they saw the man liberated and transformed. They were stricken with fear. What had held them together was their tight grip on power, privilege, and sanity; all of that had been shaken, challenged, and exposed. To keep things the way they were used to, they begged Jesus to leave. They didn't want to make room for the man to belong anywhere other than the tombs, outside of the norm, the privileged, the "righteous collective."

Scapegoating

In other words, they made him a scapegoat, which was a convenient way of releasing and transferring their well-defended sense of shame, guilt, and fear onto another and giving them a collective unanimity against a chosen victim. It gave them security and peace, and optically gave a false sense of community and strength that was "built upon the lies about the guilt of the victim and the innocence of the collective."[4]

Too often, this same tactic has been used toward the queer community. The ever-reliable arsenal use of the "clobber texts" (Genesis 19; Lev. 18:22; Rom. 1:26–27; 1 Cor. 6:9 and 1 Tim. 1:10) are used as scriptural prohibitions to force conformity and compliance. Appealing to scriptural authority based on a singular and rigid interpretation of a few texts becomes the battle cry—the very source of establishing evangelical unity and a feeling of certitude and pride for doing "God's work." To further guard and protect its conservative theological inheritance, heightened policing and surveillance against the queer community within the church are rigidly enforced.

Conservative Christianity holds on to these old ways of being, but our highly secularized postmodern society is witness to the rapid downturn in church attendance and allegiance as religious life increasingly recedes into the background and is relegated to the private sphere. At the same time, cultural pluralism is thriving, in the sense that individuals should question familiar scripts and reconstruct their identities based on their lived experiences. The public and private lives of individuals are also becoming more segregated. With these cultural shifts affecting all areas of life, evangelicalism continues to tighten its grip on orthodoxy as a way of solidifying control and influence on the faithful. This conservative evangelical hegemony has chosen to scapegoat the queer community with a fixed and nonnegotiable stance that renders those with differing hermeneutics and "alternative lifestyles" as an other or outsider, odd and defective heterosexuals.[5]

On an individual level, people scapegoat the queer community as a way to hide, deflect, and disown their personal frailties—a tried and useful psychological defense. By focusing on the great sin of queer sexuality, they distract themselves from or hinder their ability to look deeper into their own layers of personal woundedness. By speaking about the unrighteousness of those with same-sex or gender erotic desires, they shore up a sense of righteous indignation to cover a multitude of personal transgressions that have gone underground and undetected. Armed with biblical assertions for the "right kind of sexuality" (read: heterosexuality) and biblical justification for the condemnation of the "wrong kind of sexuality" (read: queer sexuality), an honest and humble inquiry into one's own failings and weaknesses as a human being may be an option but not as a first recourse (Matt. 7:5). This righteous anger has become a badge of honor displayed to hide a tattered soul in need of grace and healing.

They then join together, as we see in conservative churches, to fight against the created enemy to relieve themselves of their responsibility to address their personal and collective beliefs and practices that tear at the heart of what it means to live in communion one with the other. Consequently, the social order remains unchanged, even defended, and collective and personal demons are projected onto the queer community.

But what recourse do we have against all this? How can we remain "seated at the feet of Jesus, clothed and in our right mind" while others drag us to a place of shame? How might we instead lean into the gentle invitation of Jesus to discern a response befitting our identity as God's beloved queers, humanly divinized by a God who is for us and against no one at all?

Imitatio Christi

The thing about sitting at the feet of Jesus is that we get to look at him and see in his eyes a gaze of love and delight in who we are as we are, regardless of what others say. "*You* are my *beloved* sons and daughters with whom I take great delight" (Matt. 3:17; Ps. 139:14). There is something profoundly affecting about being seen without feeling judged, of receiving someone else's beholding without the need to hold back, of gradually discovering that this seeing offers an invitation to get past all the forced descriptions and imposed characterizations and opens into an invitation to see ourselves as people who are of immense value, worth, and possibility.

When we look at ourselves through these eyes, we gradually discover ourselves in a different light, as if for the first time, as delightful and loveable—just as we are. This different sort of sitting and seeing requires we keep working to clear away the scales of lies, doubts, guilt, and shame that blind us from truly seeing our sacred worth, whether those scales are imposed or internalized. God, who is always coming toward us, invites us to relax and behold our glorious, dare I say fabulous, beauty in God's own eyes.

For many, this may be difficult to hear given the onslaught of disparaging messages, hurtful and harmful politics, and disapproving looks we have heard and seen, especially from those who claim to speak for God. But God has no part in this sacred violence.

With this in mind, we rise from the ruins of exclusion and sacred violence and in faith anchor ourselves to the chief cornerstone (Eph. 2:20) with the kind of faith that refuses to be crushed, that we might be re-created by the very person who laid bare the true nature and intent of the human sacrificial system through his own crucifixion. When we sit at the feet of Jesus, we go back to the cross as the inaugural site of the promised salvation but not in the way we have always understood this sacred drama—not to hear the story that makes Jesus a scapegoat.[6] The cross was not required to appease God's vengeful intentions but happened to make plain our proclivities for "inter-human violence," to show us the damage we are capable of doing to one another.[7]

By taking the place of the customary scapegoat, Christ makes it possible for us to begin to live our lives without sacrificing the lives of others.[8] The cycle of sacred violence that keeps the legacy of the victimization alive finally has been disrupted and broken not by a will to power or subjugate but by the will to love expressed so vividly in God's gracious act of self-emptying (Phil. 2:5–11). By breaking this cycle, we also discover we are inside God's divine life, energy, and action in the world and therefore are primed to flourish as queer folk in more ways than we can ever dare to imagine (Eph. 3:20).[9]

New Creation

This new creation opened for us calls for a new, strange, and unfamiliar way of being together. Thankfully, we have been gifted with the Holy Spirit (Acts 2:38), who lives in us (Rom. 8:11), producing wisdom and revelation (Eph. 1:17) to clearly discern the ways of the cross from the ways of the world. Since we have been crucified with Christ, we are no longer held in bondage by those who choose unanimity over and against a despised other. But Christ, who lives in us, is inducting us into a new way of life in which we live by faith in him who loved us and gave himself for us (Gal. 2:20). The place of shame inhabited by Christ on the cross has also become the place where a new vision of humanity is inaugurated, an "alternative vision of what human beings could be or are meant to be."[10] This new creation has come, and the old has gone; the new is here, right now in the concreteness of our queer lives (2 Cor. 5:17).

We participate in the unfolding of new creation by redirecting our gaze from each other to Jesus Christ as the mediator of nonretaliatory, nonacquisitive, and nonviolent expressions of consummate love.

Our mindful and contemplative gaze is critical as we embark on a totally strange way of being together, especially when it comes to relating with those who have scapegoated us. At first glance, these strange and unfamiliar ways of loving might be counterintuitive for us who have been forcibly pushed to occupy places of shame because of our queer desires. But when we turn our eyes on Jesus, who looks back at us with such delight, regard, and love, we begin to shed false images of ourselves and reclaim our favored and bestowed identity in Christ. The self that is hidden in Christ makes possible a self-affirming stance amid the tendency to put on a false sense of self or to believe in false and life-negating narratives, discourse, and practices.

This, of course, takes a lot of courage. The temptation to fall back to the familiar roles of victim and perpetrator that lock all of us in an ongoing spiral of sacred violence can feel irresistible and overwhelming at times. The challenge before us lies in reclaiming our divinized humanity and nonrivalrous desires that benefit not only us but others as well.

Here, we go back to the self-emptying example of Jesus Christ (Philippians 2) whom we imitate so that his will to love is intricately woven with our own desires. This is what Paul means by having the "mind of Christ": to follow his example of self-emptying. Paul's admonition is not just about having the right belief, but also about living rightly—living in light of the pattern of Christ's cruciform love that exposes the futility and fatality of scapegoating and that initiates radical hospitality and openness with ourselves and others.[11]

This new way of being together confirms our participation in the life of God. As we go deeper into this divine life by remaining connected to the vine (John 15:4), we gradually habituate Christ's own desires. His took the "downward path of dishonor, suffering, and self-renouncing love," which was his way of entering the depths of human vulnerability, experiencing the very depths of our own brokenness, suffering, and alienation.[12]

For many, Christ's identification with us may be difficult to grasp. After all, we have been made to believe that our banishment from the circle of the sacred is sanctioned by God, and so, instead of experiencing accompaniment in times of despair, we have only known absence and abandonment. We have incurred so much anger, disbelief, bewilderment, incalculable pain, isolation, and even trauma because of the bonds, emotional connections, and spiritual ties we have worked so hard to establish and possess by virtue of being human have been severed so effortlessly.

Know that I make no judgment for a gamut of feelings evoked by the claim that Christ identifies with us in that familiar place of shame. None at all. Nor is this assertion being forced on any of us. Whatever it is that we feel or think, Christ's decision to love us precedes all that. Even at our weakest or in moments of unbelief, his forgiving heart and tender loving gaze remain unchanged. Why? Because God has no part in our banishment and instead comes to us to heal our fragmented selves, help us remember our sacred worth, restore our place in God's queerdom, and God chooses us to participate in the flourishing of it all, even in those who drove us into exile.

Since God is not part of the established sacred order—and, in fact, came to dismantle it (Matt. 12:17–21)—we can reimagine Christ as the one searching for those of us who have been exiled and scattered; the Good Shepherd will feed and care for us.[13] Christ is the one who comes looking for us among the tombs. And when our bruised and broken selves are found by him, even our resistance to be touched, soothed, and held will not be met by displeasure or disappointment, but with empathy, validation, comfort, and an overflowing desire to heal and restore us.

The celebration of the Eucharist as a symbolic meal is an ongoing invitation for us to participate in the ministry of reconciliation (2 Cor. 5:18), to reflect through our life together the spirit of sharing and unity in Christ, and to subvert any attempts at sacrificing others on the altar of sacred violence. For queer Christians, the Eucharist is also a space for a "heart close to cracking," a space where we begin to understand that God has nothing to do with the violence inflicted on us because of who we are and whom we love.[14] As an expression of solidarity with those victimized by this sacred order, Christ occupied that place of shame to finally reveal its human origins and transform that very same place into a space where life can begin anew.

With Christ present as the "crucified one, and we as penitents learning to step out of solidarity with our multiple and varied modes of complicity in crucifixion," we come to the table set before us by our host and model with thanksgiving to claim our place as "co-participators in an unimagined creation."[15] Yes, you and I have been lifted from this place of shame and are now called into being by God, who likes and takes delights in us as we are. Perhaps God is a little giddy as well to see who we could be and might become as recipients of this vivacious and creative force at work in us and all of creation. So we take all that with us, lean into the experience of being summoned to an intimate table fellowship with God, and make use of it as nourishment as we pattern our desires after the eucharistic life similar to that of Jesus Christ, our model and mediator of God's own victimless desires.

And so we continue to sit at the feet of Jesus, clothed, and in our right mind . . . because that is what we do and that is who we are: queer divine.

ACKNOWLEDGMENTS

I may not be a biblical scholar, but I love the Word, the Living Word, who shapeshifts in the form of ordinary beings whose accompaniment throughout the writing of this book became a source of laughter, inspiration, challenge, discovery, and delight.

Thank you to my Ru'Me crew in Winnipeg, Manitoba, whose ordinary acts of kindness and hospitality (i.e., taking care of domestic necessities) gave me the time and space so I can focus on writing. Their quiet confidence and belief in me (and a steady supply of my fave Filipino cuisines) buoyed my spirit and body when it needed an uplift and nourishment.

My colleague and friend Dong Hyeon Jeong received screenshots of paragraphs I had written and messaged me back with words and emojis of encouragement, and offered other queer ways of interpreting these parables. I am also grateful for K. K. Yeoh, a giant in New Testament studies, for his gracious feedback on the introduction.

My siblings, all queer-identifying UMC clergy people of color, offered so much honesty, vulnerability, courage, tears, and hope as they shared their stories with me. Their lives and loves touched mine so profoundly that I held onto them as I queered these parables. The opportunity to hear these stories came because of a grant I received from the Louisville Institute, whose generosity allowed me to center the voices of my queer siblings through this book.

My colleagues and friends at the Wabash Center for Teaching and Learning in Theology and Religion through the leadership of Nancy Lynne Westfield invited me to take part in their Writing Inaugural Workshop, where I wrote and received creative inputs on one of the chapters in the book.

Thank you to my editor, Milton Brasher-Cunningham, and the editorial team at Church Publishing, whose patience and gentle nudges kept me focused to get this book in your hands.

I wrote this book during this pandemic time, and there wasn't a day when I did not feel deeply held and cared for by another Other, the Word, the Living Word who loves me as I am, queer and all.

In Christi Gloriam.

NOTES

Introduction

1 Halperin, *Saint Foucault*, 17.

2 See, for example, Bailey, Liew, and Segovia, *They Were All Together in One Place*; Stone, *Queer Commentary and the Hebrew Bible*; and Goss and West, *Take Back the Word*.

3 Randolf, in Anderson, *Ancient Laws and Contemporary Controversies*, 7.

4 Anderson, *Ancient Laws and Contemporary Controversies*, 8.

5 Menendez-Antuña, "Is There a Room for Queer Desires?" 400.

6 Stewart, "LGBT/Queer Hermeneutics and the Hebrew Bible," 290.

7 Altheus-Reid, *Queer God*, 146.

8 Koch, quoted in Greenough, *Queer Theologies*, 96.

9 Gafney, *Womanist Midrash*, 4.

10 Stewart, "LGBT/Queer Hermeneutics and the Hebrew Bible," 289–314.

11 Punt, "Sex and Gender, and Liminality in Biblical Texts," 382–98.

12 Alison, *Broken Hearts and New Creations*, 269.

13 Ricoeur, *Interpretation Theory*, 74.

14 Stewart, "The Hermeneutics of Suspicion," 296–307.

15 Ricoeur, *Interpretation Theory*, 76–77.

16 Abraham, "On the Doorstep of the Work," 5.

17 Ricoeur, in Abraham, "Appropriation," 7.

18 Greenough, *Queer Theologies*, 107.

19 Snodgrass, *Stories with Intent*, loc. 318; Dodd, in Snodgrass, *Stories with Intent*, loc. 268; Hong, in Snodgrass, *Stories with Intent*, loc. 283; Snodgrass, *Stories with Intent*, loc. 318.

20 Snodgrass, *Stories with Intent*, loc. 162; Snodgrass, *Stories with Intent*, loc. 160.

Chapter 1

1 Bailey, *Good Shepherd*, 278.

2 Bailey, *Good Shepherd*, 270.

3 Bailey, *Good Shepherd*, 281.

4 Bailey, *Good Shepherd*, 274.

5 Bailey, *Good Shepherd*, 275.

6 Thomson quoted in Bailey, *Good Shepherd*, 278.

7 Stanley (Lectures on the History of the Easter Church) in Bailey, *Good Shepherd*, 24.

8 Schaff (History of Christian Church) in Bailey, *Good Shepherd*, 24.

9 Kazen, *Emotions in Biblical Law*, 93.

10 Ahmed, *Cultural Politics of Emotion*, 147.

11 Nolasco, *God's Beloved Queer*, 8.

12 Nolasco, *God's Beloved Queer*, 76–77.

13 Flemming, *Philippians*, 114.

14 Alison, *Faith beyond Resentment*, 115–16.

Chapter 2

1 Keesmat, in Longenecker, *Challenge of Jesus Parables*, 265.

2 Bailey, *Poet and Peasant and Through the Peasant Eyes*, 506–7.

3 Bailey, *Poet and Peasant and Through the Peasant Eyes*, 515.

4 Bailey, *Poet and Peasant and Through the Peasant Eyes*, 534.

5 Snodgrass, *Stories with Intent*, loc. 7388.

6 Marshall, in Bailey, *Poet and Peasant and Through the Peasant Eyes*, 590.

7 Gutiérrez, *Theology of Liberation*, xxvi.

8 Bailey, *Poet and Peasant and Through the Peasant Eyes*, 539.

9 Nolasco, *Contemplative Counselor*, 100.

10 Merton, *Contemplative Prayer*, 33.

11 Nolasco, *Contemplative Counselor*, 115.

12 St. John of the Cross, *Ascent of Mount Carmel*, 55.

13 Alison, *On Being Liked*, 12.

Chapter 3

1 Levine, *Short Stories by Jesus*, 148.

2 Snodgrass, *Stories with Intent*, loc. 5219.

3 Levine, *Short Stories by Jesus*, 151.

4 Scott, *Hear Then the Parable*, 380.

5 Funk, "The Looking Glass Tree Is for the Birds," 7.

6 Funk, "The Looking Glass Tree Is for the Birds," 7.

7 Funk, "The Looking Glass Tree Is for the Birds," 7.

8 Zimmerman, *Puzzling the Parables of Jesus*, 258.

9 Nolasco, *God's Beloved Queer*, 2.

10 Snodgrass, *Stories with Intent*, loc. 5348.

11 Zimmerman, *Puzzling the Parables of Jesus*, 241.

12 Zimmerman, *Puzzling the Parables of Jesus*, 250.

13 National Alliance on Mental Illness, "LGBTQI," Nami. https://www.nami.org/Your-Journey/ Identity-and-Cultural-Dimensions/LGBTQI.

14 Nolasco, *God's Beloved Queer*, 92.

15 Nolasco, *God's Beloved Queer*, 92.

16 Adams, "Loving Mimesis," 277.

17 Volf, "Human Flourishing," 24.

Chapter 4

1 Snodgrass, *Stories with Intent*, loc. 5731.

2 Crossan, *Finding Is the First Act*, 77.

3 Derett, *Law in the New Testament*, 6–9 .

4 Jeremias, in Scott, *Hear Then the Parable*, 401.

5 Jeremias, in Scott, *Hear Then the Parable*, 401.

6 Roberts, in Johnson, "Joy: A Review," 5.

7 Fredrickson, in Johnson, "Joy: A Review," 6.

8 Taylor, *Cruelty*, 131.

9 Taylor, *Cruelty*, 131.

10 Mitchell, "Art of Ridicule," 1.

11 Tomkins, in Nathanson, *Shame and Pride*, 134.

12 Meadows, in Johnson, "Joy: A Review," 7.

13 Meadows, in Johnson, "Joy: A Review," 8.

14 Mitchell, "Art of Ridicule," 1.

15 brown, *Pleasure Activism*, 10.

Chapter 5

1 Snodgrass, *Stories with Intent*, loc. 3638.

2 Snodgrass, *Stories with Intent*, loc. 3671.

3 Snodgrass, *Stories with Intent*, loc. 3702, 3769.

4 Snodgrass, *Stories with Intent*, loc. 3885.

5 Nolasco, *God's Beloved Queer*, 36.

6 Browne, in Formby, "LGBT 'Communities,'" 11.

7 Neff, *Self-Compassion*, 47.

8 Formby, "LGBT 'Communities,'" 7.

9 Sanger and Taylor, *Mapping Intimacies*, 2.

10 Formby, "LGBT 'Communities,'" 11.

11 Browne, *Queer Spiritual Spaces*, 2.

12 Jensen, in Formby, "LGBT 'Communities,'" 21.

13 Nolasco, *Compassionate Presence*, 72.

14 Happold, *Mysticism*, 70.

15 Finley, *Awakening Call*, 76.

16 Nolasco, *God's Beloved Queer*, 108–109.

17 Tip, in Formby, "LGBT 'Communities,'" 37ff.

18 Tip, in Formby, "LGBT 'Communities,'" 49.

Chapter 6

1 Green, *Gospel of Luke*, 474.

2 Green, *Dictionary of Jesus and the Gospels*, 474.

3 Lancaster, "New Wine and Old Wineskins," Beth Immanuel
  Messianic Synagogue, https://www.bethimmanuel.org/articles/
  new-wine-and-old-wineskins-parable-luke-536-39-re-examined.

4 Ibid.

5 Green, *Dictionary of Jesus and the Gospels*, 482.

6 Ibid.

7 Kruks, in Zajicek, Shields, and Wright, "Bringing the Body Back," 244.

8 Beauvoir, in Zeiler, "A Phenomenology of Excorporation, Bodily Alienation, and Resistance," 71.

9 Ritzer, in Zajicek, Shields, and Wright, "Bringing the Body Back," 245.

10 Sullivan, in Turner, *Handbook of Body Studies*, 291.

11 Foucault, in Turner, *Handbook of Body Studies*, 293.

12 Zajicek, Shields, and Wright, "Bringing the Body Back," 242.

13 Alison, *Jesus the Forgiving Victim*, 19.

14 Zeiler, "A Phenomenology of Excorporation, Bodily Alienation, and Resistance," 71; Ahmed, *Queer Phenomenology*, 7.

15 Ahmed, *Queer Phenomenology*, 4, 14.

16 Davis, *Handbook of Gender and Women Studies*, 311.

17 Butler, "Performative Acts," 519.

18 Kinsman, *Regulation of Desire*, 62.

19 Alison, *Broken Hearts and New Creations*, 269.

20 Ruti, "Disenchanted," 17.

Chapter 7

1 Bailey, *Finding the Lost Cultural Keys to Luke 15*, 170.

2 Bailey, *Finding the Lost Cultural Keys to Luke 15*, 171.

3 Bailey, *Finding the Lost Cultural Keys to Luke 15*, 183.

4 Bailey, *Finding the Lost Cultural Keys to Luke 15*, 181.

5 Bailey, *Finding the Lost Cultural Keys to Luke 15*, 189.

6 Bailey, *Finding the Lost Cultural Keys to Luke 15*, 190.

7 Ibn al-Tayyib, in Bailey, *Finding the Lost Cultural Keys to Luke 15*, 193.

8 Ibn al-Tayyib, in Bailey, *Finding the Lost Cultural Keys to Luke 15*, 196.

9 Bailey, *Finding the Lost Cultural Keys to Luke 15*, 201.

10 Bailey, *Finding the Lost Cultural Keys to Luke 15*, 265.

11 Lachs, in Bailey, *Finding the Lost Cultural Keys to Luke 15*, 173.

12 Bailey, *Finding the Lost Cultural Keys to Luke 15*, 176.

13 Nouwen, *Return of the Prodigal Son*, 44.

14 Bailey, *Finding the Lost Cultural Keys to Luke 15*, 216.
15 Bailey, *Finding the Lost Cultural Keys to Luke 15*, 217.
16 Bailey, *Finding the Lost Cultural Keys to Luke 15*, 223.
17 Bailey, *Finding the Lost Cultural Keys to Luke 15*, 234.
18 Bailey, *Finding the Lost Cultural Keys to Luke 15*, 279.
19 Bailey, *Finding the Lost Cultural Keys to Luke 15*, 273.

Chapter 8

1 Watkins, *Towards Psychologies of Liberation*, 64.
2 Grimsrud, "Scapegoating No More," 50; Schwagger, *Must There Be Scapegoats?* 66–67.
3 Nadella, *Dialogue Not Dogma*, 72.
4 Just, *Luke 9:51–24:53 (Concordia Commentary)*, 452.
5 Grimsrud, "Scapegoating No More," 56.

Chapter 9

1 Snodgrass, *Stories with Intent*, loc. 12487.
2 Snodgrass, *Stories with Intent*, loc. 12480.
3 Scott, *Hear Then the Parable*, 226
4 Scott, *Hear Then the Parable*, 226.
5 Scott, *Hear Then the Parable*, 227.
6 Snodgrass, *Stories with Intent*, loc. 12579.
7 Scott, *Hear Then the Parable*, 226.
8 Scott, *Hear Then the Parable*, 228.
9 Scott, *Hear Then the Parable*, 230.
10 Scott, *Hear Then the Parable*, 235.
11 Taylor, *Cruelty*, 149.
12 Noor, Chee, and Ahmad, "Is There a Gay Advantage in Creativity?" 32.
13 Charyton, "What Is the Relationship Between Sexual Orientation, Bisexuality and Creativity?" 49–69.
14 "Unlocking Your Queer Creative Power."
15 Snodgrass, *Stories with Intent*, loc. 12600.

Chapter 10

1 Bailey, *Jesus through Middle Eastern Eyes*, 285.
2 Bohache, "Embodiment as Incarnation," 9.
3 Nolasco, *God's Beloved Queer*, 2.
4 Goss, *Jesus Acted Up*, 64.
5 Hellwig, in Isherwood, "Queering Christ," 253.
6 Alison, *On Being Liked*, 22.
7 Isherwood, "Queering Christ," 254.
8 Isherwood, "Queering Christ," 254–25.
9 Isherwood, "Queering Christ," 252.
10 Isherwood, "Queering Christ," 255.
11 Isherwood, "Queering Christ," 250.
12 Alison, *Jesus the Forgiving Victim*, 234.
13 Adams, "Loving Mimesis," 277.
14 Adams, "Loving Mimesis," 289.
15 Grimsrud, "Scapegoating No More," 52.
16 Flemming, *Philippians*, 114.
17 Bailey, *Jesus through Middle Eastern Eyes*, 282.

Epilogue

1 This is an adaptation of a sermon I preached weeks after the Special General Conference held in St. Louis, Missouri, in February 2019. It also contains ideas and core themes lifted from my book *God's Beloved Queer*, published later that year.
2 Alison, *Faith beyond Resentment*, 125.
3 Alison, *Faith beyond Resentment*, 126.
4 Colloquium, "What Is Mimetic Theory?" 1.
5 Vasey-Suanders, *Scandals of Evangelicals and Homosexuality*, 40, 54, 73–99.
6 Alison, *Knowing Jesus*, 36.
7 Grimsrud, "Scapegoating No More," 52.
8 Grimsrud, "Scapegoating No More," 52.
9 Alison, *Undergoing God*, 2–3.
10 Adams, "Loving Mimesis," 277.

11 Adams, "Loving Mimesis," 141, 295; Flemming, *Philippians*, 112.

12 Flemming, *Philippians*, 114.

13 Flemming, *Philippians*, 115.

14 Alison, *Faith beyond Resentment*, 34.

15 Alison, *Faith beyond Resentment*, 34, 123.

BIBLIOGRAPHY

Abraham, Ibrahim. "On the Doorstep of the Work: Ricoroeurian Hermeneutics, Queer Hermeneutics, Queer Hermeneutics and Scripture." *Bible and Critical Theory* 3, no. 1 (2007): 4.1–4.12.

———. "Appropriation." *The Bible and Critical Theory* 3, no. 1 (2007): 4.7, doi:10.2104/bc070004.

Adam, Rebecca. "Loving Mimesis and Girard's 'Scapegoat of the Text': A Creative Reassessment of Mimetic Desire." In *Violence Renounced: René Girard, Biblical Studies, and Peacemaking*, edited by Willard M. Swartley, 277–307. Telford, ON: Pandora, 2000.

Ahmed, Sarah. *The Cultural Politics of Emotion*. New York: Routledge, 2004.

———. *Queer Phenomenology: Orientations, Objects, and Others*. Durham, NC: Duke University Press, 2016.

Alison, James. *Broken Hearts and New Creations*. London: Continuum, 2010.

———. *Faith beyond Resentment: Fragments Catholic and Gay*. New York: Crossroad, 2015.

———. *Jesus the Forgiving Victim: Listening for the Unheard Voices*. Glenview, IL: Doers, 2013.

———. *Knowing Jesus*. London: SPCK Classics, 2012.

———. *On Being Liked*. New York: Crossroad, 2016.

———. *Undergoing God: Dispatches from the Scene of a Break-In*. London: Continuum, 2006.

Altheus-Reid, Marcella. *The Queer God*. New York: Routledge, 2003.

Anderson, Cheryl. *Ancient Laws and Contemporary Controversies*. Oxford: Oxford University Press, 2009.

Bailey, Kenneth B. *Finding the Lost Key Cultural Keys to Luke 15.* St. Louis, MO: Concordia, 1992.

———. *The Good Shepherd: A Thousand-Year Journey from Psalm 23 to the New Testament.* Downers Grove, IL: IVP, 2014.

———. *Jesus through Middle Eastern Eyes: Cultural Studies in the Gospels.* Downers Grove, IL: IVP Academic, 2008.

———. *Poet and Peasant and Through the Peasant Eyes: A Literary-Cultural Approach to the Parables in Luke.* Combined ed. Grand Rapids, MI: Eerdmans, 1983.

Bailey, Randall C., Tat-Siong Benny Liew, and Fernando F. Segovia. *They Were All Together in One Place: Toward Minority Biblical Criticism.* New York: Society of Biblical Literature Semeia Studies, 2009.

Bohache, Thomas. "Embodiment as Incarnation: An Incipient Queer Christology." *Theology & Sexuality* 10, no. 1 (2003): 9–29.

brown, adrienne maree. *Pleasure Activism: The Politics of Feeling Good.* Oakland, CA: AK Press, 2019.

Browne, Kath, et al. *Queer Spiritual Spaces: Sexuality and Sacred Spaces.* Surrey, UK: Ashgate, 2010.

Butler, Judith. "Performative Acts and Gender Constitution: An Essay in Phenomenology and Feminist Theory." *Theatre Journal* 40, no. 4 (1988): 519–31.

Charyton, Christine. "What Is the Relationship Between Sexual Orientation, Bisexuality and Creativity?" *Journal of Bisexuality* 6, no. 4 (2007): 49–69.

Crossan, John Dominic. *Finding Is the First Act: Trove Folktales and Jesus' Treasure Parable.* Eugene, OR: Wipf and Stock, 2008.

Davis, Kathy, et. al. *Handbook of Gender and Women's Studies.* Thousand Oaks, CA: Sage, 2006.

Derrett, J. Duncan M. *Law in the New Testament.* Eugene, OR: Wipf and Stock, 2005.

Finley, James. *The Awakening Call: Fostering Intimacy with God.* Notre Dame, IN: Ave Maria, 1984.

Flemming, Dean. *Philippians: A Commentary in the Wesleyan Tradition.* Kansas City, MO: Beacon Hill, 2009.

Formby, Eleanor. "LGBT 'Communities' and the (Self-)regulation and Shaping of Intimacy." *Sociological Research Online* 27, no. 1 (2022): 8–26.

Funk, Robert. "The Looking-Glass Tree Is for the Birds." *Interpretation* 27, no. 1 (January 1973): 3–9.

Gafney, Wilda C. *Womanist Midrash: A Reintroduction to the Women of the Torah and the Throne.* Louisville, KY: Westminster, 2017.

Goss, Robert. *Jesus Acted Up: A Gay and Lesbian Manifesto.* New York: HarperCollins, 1994.

Goss, Robert, and Monica West. *Take Back the Word: A Queer Reading of the Bible.* Cleveland, OH: Pilgrim Press, 2000.

Green, Joel. *Dictionary of Jesus and the Gospels.* Downers Grove, IL: InterVarsity Press, 1992.

Green, Joel B. *The Gospel of Luke.* Grand Rapids, MI: Eerdmans, 1997.

Greenough, Chris. *Queer Theologies: The Basics.* New York: Routledge, 2019.

Grimsrud, Ted. "Scapegoating No More: Christian Pacifism and New Testament View of Jesus Death." In *Violence Renounced: René Girard, Biblical Studies, and Peacemaking,* edited by Willard M. Swartley, 49–69. Telford, PA: Pandora, 2000.

Gutiérrez, Gustavo. *A Theology of Liberation: History, Politics, and Salvation.* Maryknoll, NY: Orbis Books, 1988.

Halperin, David. *Saint Foucault: Towards A Gay Hagiography.* Oxford: Oxford University Press, 1997.

Happold, F. C. *Mysticism: A Study and an Anthology.* London: Penguin, 1973.

Isherwood, Lisa. "Queering Christ: Outrageous Acts and Theological Rebellions." *Literature and Theology* 15, no. 3 (2001): 249–61.

John of the Cross. *The Ascent of Mount Carmel and the Dark Night.* Translated by John Vanard. Darlington, UK: Darlington Carmel, 1981.

Johnson, Matthew Kuan. "Joy: A Review of the Literature and Suggestions for Future Directions." *The Journal of Positive Psychology* 15, no. 1 (2020): 5–24.

Just, Arthur. *Luke 9:51–24:53 (Concordia Commentary).* St. Louis, MO: Concordia, 1997.

Kazen, Thomas. *Emotions in Biblical Law: A Cognitive Science Approach.* Sheffield: Sheffield Phoenix, 2011.

Kinsman, Gary. *The Regulation of Desire: Homo and Hetero Sexualities.* 2nd ed. New York: Black Rose, 1992.

Lachs, S. T. *A Rabbinic Commentary on the New Testament (The Gospels of Matthew, Mark, and Luke).* Hoboken, NJ: KTAC Publishing House, 1987.

Lancaster, D. T. "New Wine and Old Wineskins." Beth Immanuel Messianic Synagogue. www.bethimmanuel.org/articles/new-wine-and-old-wineskins-parable-luke-536-39-re-examined.

Levine, Amy-Jill. *Short Stories by Jesus: The Enigmatic Parables of a Controversial Rabbi.* New York: HarperOne, 2014.

Longenecker, Richard, ed. *The Challenge of Jesus' Parables.* Grand Rapids, MI: Eerdmans, 2000.

Marshall, I. H. "Luke xvi 8—Who Condemned the Unjust Steward?" *JTS N.S.* 19 (1968): 617–19.

Menéndez-Antuña, Luis. "Is There a Room for Queer Desires? A Methodological Reflection on Queer Desires in the Context of Contemporary New Testament Studies." *Biblical Interpretation* 23, no. 3 (2015): 399–427.

Merton, Thomas. *The Contemplative Prayer.* London: Darton, Longman & Todd, 1969.

Mitchell, Reagan Patrick. "The Art of Ridicule: Black Queer Joy in the Face of the Fatigues." *International Journal of Qualitative Studies in Education* 35, no. 2 (2022): 1–17.

Nadella, Raj. *Dialogue Not Dogma: Many Voices in the Gospel of Luke.* Edinburgh: T&T Clark, 2011.

Nathanson, Donald L. *Shame and Pride: Affect, Sex, and the Birth of the Self.* New York: W. W. Norton, 1994.

Neff, Kristen. *Self-Compassion: Stop Beating Yourself Up and Leave Insecurity Behind.* New York: HarperCollins, 2011.

Nolasco, Rolf. *The Compassionate Presence: A Radical Response to Human Suffering.* Eugene, OR: Cascade, 2016.

———. *The Contemplative Counselor: A Way of Being.* Minneapolis: Fortress Press, 2011.

———. *God's Beloved Queer: Identity, Spirituality, and Practice.* Eugene, OR: Wipf & Stock, 2019.

Noor, Amelia Mohd, Chew Sim Chee, and Aslina Ahmad. "Is There a Gay Advantage in Creativity?" *International Journal of Psychological Studies* 5 (2013): 32.

Nouwen, Henri J. M. *The Return of the Prodigal Son: A Story of Homecoming.* New York: Image Books, 1992.

Punt, Jeremy. "Sex and Gender, and Liminality in Biblical Texts: Venturing into Postcolonial Queer Biblical Interpretation." *Neotestamentica* 41, no. 2 (2007): 382–98.

Ricoeur, Paul. *Figuring the Sacred: Religion, Narrative, and Imagination.* Minneapolis: Fortress Press, 1995.

———. *Interpretation Theory: Discourse and the Surplus of Meaning.* 1st ed. Austin: Texas Christian University Press, 1976.

Ruti, Mari. "The Disenchanted: Queer Theory Between Negativity and Flourishing." Das Unbehagen. December 16, 2017. http://dasunbehagen.org/day-mari-ruti/.

Sanger, Tam, and Yvette Taylor, eds. *Mapping Intimacies: Relations, Exchanges, Affects.* New York: Palgrave Macmillan, 2013.

Schaff, Philip. *History of the Christian Church.* Peabody, MA: Hendrickson, 2002.

Schwagger, Raymund. *Must There Be Scapegoats? Violence and Redemption in the Bible.* San Francisco: Harper & Row, 1987.

Scott, Bernard B. *Hear Then the Parable: A Commentary on the Parables of Jesus.* Minneapolis: Fortress Press, 1989.

Snodgrass, Klyne. *Stories with Intent: A Comprehensive Guide to the Parables of Jesus.* Grand Rapids, MI: Eerdmans, 2008.

Stanley, Arthur P. *Lectures on the History of the Eastern Church.* Neuilly-sur-Seine, France: Ulan Press, 2012.

Stewart, David. "The Hermeneutics of Suspicion." *Literature and Theology.* 3, no. 3 (1989): 296–307.

Stewart, Tabb D. "LGBT/Queer Hermeneutics and the Hebrew Bible." *Currents in Biblical Research* 15, no. 3 (2017): 289–314.

Stone, Ken. *Queer Commentary and the Hebrew Bible.* Cleveland, OH: Pilgrim Press, 2002.

Taylor, Kathleen. *Cruelty: Human Evil and the Human Brain.* Oxford: Oxford University Press, 2009.

Thomson, W. C. *Land the Book.* New Delhi: Facsimile Publisher, 2016.

Turner, Bryan S. *Routledge Handbook of Body Studies.* New York: Routledge, 2012.

"Unlocking Your Queer Creative Power." https://blog.lighthouse.lgbt/unlocking-your-queer-creative-power/.

Vasey-Saunders, Mark. *The Scandals of Evangelicals and Homosexuality, English Evangelical Texts,* 1960–2010. Surrey: Ashgate, 2015.

Volf, Miroslav. "Human Flourishing." In *Renewing the Evangelical Mission*, edited by Richard Lints, 13–30. Grand Rapids, MI: Eerdmans, 2013.

Watkins, Mary, and Helene Shulman. *Towards Psychologies of Liberation.* New York: Palgrave Macmillan, 2008.

Weedon, Chris. *Feminist Practice and Poststructuralist Theory.* 2nd ed. Hoboken, NJ: Wiley-Blackwell, 1996.

"What is Mimetic Theory?" https://violenceandreligion.com/mimetic-theory/.

Zajicek, Anna M., Chris Shields, and Joe L. Wright. "Bringing The Body Back In: The Social Construction of Embodied Sexual Identities." *Social Thought & Research* 24, no. 1/2 (2001): 237–68.

Zeiler, Kristin. "A Phenomenology of Excorporation, Bodily Alienation, and Resistance: Rethinking Sexed and Racialized Embodiment." *Hypatia* 28, no. 1 (2013): 69–84.

Zimmermann, Ruben. *Puzzling the Parables of Jesus: Methods and Interpretation.* Minneapolis: Fortress Press, 2015.

CPSIA information can be obtained
at www.ICGtesting.com
Printed in the USA
JSHW020921270822
29802JS00004B/4

9 781640 653658